Contemporary Research on Police Organizations

T0331388

Much research on policing focuses on individual officer decision making in the field, but officers are positioned within organizations. Organizational characteristics, including structures, policies, management, training, culture, traditions, and the environmental context affect individual officer behavior and attitudes. Recent high-profile controversies surrounding policing have generated interest in examining what factors may have led to current crises.

In this book, contributors discuss how police department priorities are made; how departments respond to sexual assault complaints; how forensic scientists deal with job stress and satisfaction; how police use gun crime incident reviews for problem solving and information sharing; how police officers view the use of body-worn cameras given their perceptions of organizational justice; and how officers view their work culture. The purpose of this book is to give policy makers and scholars some guidance on the interplay between the individual and the organization. By understanding this dynamic, police administrators should be able to better devise reform efforts.

This book was originally published as a special issue of the *Journal of Crime and Justice*.

George W. Burruss is an associate professor in the Department of Criminology at the University of South Florida and the Florida Center for Cybersecurity, USA.

Matthew J. Giblin is professor in the Department of Criminology and Criminal Justice at Southern Illinois University, Carbondale, USA.

Joseph A. Schafer is professor in the Department of Criminology and Criminal Justice at Southern Illinois University, Carbondale, USA.

Contemporary Research on Police Organizations

Edited by
George W. Burruss, Matthew J. Giblin and Joseph A. Schafer

Routledge
Taylor & Francis Group

LONDON AND NEW YORK

First published 2018 by Routledge

2 Park Square, Milton Park, Abingdon, Oxfordshire OX14 4RN
52 Vanderbilt Avenue, New York, NY 10017

Routledge is an imprint of the Taylor & Francis Group, an informa business

First issued in paperback 2020

British Library Cataloguing in Publication Data
A catalogue record for this book is available from the British Library

ISBN 13: 978-1-138-49402-2 (hbk)
ISBN 13: 978-0-367-58967-7 (pbk)

Typeset in Myriad Pro
by RefineCatch Limited, Bungay, Suffolk

Publisher's Note
The publisher accepts responsibility for any inconsistencies that may have arisen during the conversion of this book from journal articles to book chapters, namely the possible inclusion of journal terminology.

Disclaimer
Every effort has been made to contact copyright holders for their permission to reprint material in this book. The publishers would be grateful to hear from any copyright holder who is not here acknowledged and will undertake to rectify any errors or omissions in future editions of this book.

Contents

Citation Information

The chapters in this book were originally published in the *Journal of Crime and Justice*, volume 40, issue 1 (March 2017). When citing this material, please use the original page numbering for each article, as follows:

Editorial

Introduction to the special issue on police organizations
George W. Burruss, Matthew J. Giblin and Joseph A. Schafer
Journal of Crime and Justice, volume 40, issue 1 (March 2017), pp. 1–4

Chapter 1

How perceptions of the institutional environment shape organizational priorities: findings from a survey of police chiefs
Matthew C. Matusiak, William R. King and Edward R. Maguire
Journal of Crime and Justice, volume 40, issue 1 (March 2017), pp. 5–19

Chapter 2

Active representation and police response to sexual assault complaints
Melissa Schaefer Morabito, April Pattavina and Linda M. Williams
Journal of Crime and Justice, volume 40, issue 1 (March 2017), pp. 20–33

Chapter 3

Examining the impact of organizational and individual characteristics on forensic scientists' job stress and satisfaction
Thomas J. Holt, Kristie R. Blevins and Ruth Waddell Smith
Journal of Crime and Justice, volume 40, issue 1 (March 2017), pp. 34–49

Chapter 4

Gun crime incident reviews as a strategy for enhancing problem solving and information sharing
Natalie Kroovand Hipple, Edmund F. McGarrell, Mallory O'Brien and Beth M. Huebner
Journal of Crime and Justice, volume 40, issue 1 (March 2017), pp. 50–67

Chapter 5

The impact of law enforcement officer perceptions of organizational justice on their attitudes regarding body-worn cameras
Michael J. Kyle and David R. White
Journal of Crime and Justice, volume 40, issue 1 (March 2017), pp. 68–83

Chapter 6
Understanding the culture of craft: lessons from two police agencies
James J. Willis and Stephen D. Mastrofski
Journal of Crime and Justice, volume 40, issue 1 (March 2017), pp. 84–100

For any permission-related enquiries please visit:
http://www.tandfonline.com/page/help/permissions

Notes on Contributors

Kristie R. Blevins is associate professor in the School of Justice Studies at Eastern Kentucky University, USA.

George W. Burruss is associate professor in the Department of Criminology at the University of South Florida and the Florida Center for Cybersecurity, USA.

Matthew J. Giblin is professor in the Department of Criminology and Criminal Justice at Southern Illinois University, Carbondale, USA.

Natalie Kroovand Hipple is assistant professor in the Department of Criminal Justice at Indiana University, USA.

Thomas J. Holt is professor in the School of Criminal Justice at Michigan State University, USA.

Beth M. Huebner is professor and graduate director in the Department of Criminology and Criminal Justice at the University of Missouri – St Louis, USA.

William R. King is professor and associate dean of Research in the College of Criminal Justice at Sam Houston State University, USA.

Michael J. Kyle is a PhD candidate in the Department of Criminology and Criminal Justice at Southern Illinois University, Carbondale, USA.

Edward R. Maguire is professor in the School of Criminology and Criminal Justice at Arizona State University, USA.

Stephen D. Mastrofski is professor in the Department of Criminology, Law and Society and director of the Center for Justice Leadership and Management at George Mason University, USA.

Matthew C. Matusiak is assistant professor in the Department of Criminal Justice at the University of Central Florida, Orlando, USA.

Edmund F. McGarrell is professor in the School of Criminal Justice at Michigan State University, USA.

Melissa Schaefer Morabito is associate professor and an associate at the Center for Women & Work in the School of Criminology and Justice Studies at the University of Massachusetts Lowell, USA.

Mallory O'Brien is assistant professor in the Institute for Health and Society at the Medical College of Wisconsin, USA.

April Pattavina is associate professor in the School of Criminology and Justice Studies at the University of Massachusetts Lowell, USA.

Joseph A. Schafer is professor in the Department of Criminology and Criminal Justice at Southern Illinois University, Carbondale, USA.

Ruth Waddell Smith is associate professor in the Forensic Science Program, within the School of Criminal Justice, at Michigan State University, USA.

David R. White is a doctoral student in the Department of Criminology and Criminal Justice at Southern Illinois University, Carbondale, USA.

Linda M. Williams is the senior research scientist and director of the Justice and Gender-Based Violence Research initiative at Wellesley Centers for Women, Wellesley College, USA.

James J. Willis is associate professor in the Department of Criminology, Law and Society, and associate director of the Center for Justice Leadership and Management at George Mason University, USA.

Introduction: thinking about police organizations

Nearly two centuries ago, the British Parliament established the legal basis for the London Metropolitan Police Department by passing the Metropolitan Police Act of 1829 (Klockars 1985; Uchida 1997). The department's first commissioners, Charles Rowan and Richard Mayne, faced the extensive task of creating an operational body capable of preventing crime. They decided on what would become historically critical matters such as uniforms, equipment, guiding principles, and the division of labor. According to Critchley's history of the London police (1967),

> It was decided to divide the Metropolitan district into seventeen police divisions each containing 165 men, making a grand total of nearly 3,000 … Each division was to be put in charge of an officer entitled 'superintendent,' under whom were to be four inspectors and sixteen sergeants … Each sergeant had control of nine constables (51).

Interestingly, the choice to structure the 'New Police' geographically (referred to as spatial complexity today) and to organize it vertically (referred to as vertical or hierarchical complexity) was done so without the benefit of a science of organizations. For most of the 1800s, the very period when police agencies were emerging in cities in England, the United States, and elsewhere, writers focused primarily on the challenges associated with industrialization such as labor shortages and the lack of skilled workers (Wren 1972). Two centuries later, the story is quite different. As the articles in this special issue show, not only has a field of organizational theory and behavior developed, the organization itself has also emerged as a critical focal point in policing research.

The roots of organizational theory and behavior are often traced back to three scholars writing around the turn of the twentieth century in different parts of the world, Frederick Taylor (1913), Max Weber (1946), and Henri Fayol (1949).[1] Through discussions of scientific management, bureaucracy, and administrative management, respectively, they offered prescriptions for the best way to structure and supervise work. Gulick (1937, 1) referred to these collective principles as a 'theory of organization.' Just 15 years later, noted organizations scholar Herbert Simon (1952) offered a much broader definition of 'organization theory,' including not only the structural features of organizations but also internal processes such as power, decision-making, motivation, and culture (1132–1139; see also Starbuck 2003).

Since mid-century, however, organization scholars have adopted a more precise nomenclature to identify particular study areas (Starbuck 2003). Organizational theory refers to the body of literature addressing the organization as a whole – a macro-level approach (Porter, Lawler, and Hackman 1975; Scott and Davis 2007; Tompkins 2005). Organizational theory researchers typically examine and explain variation across organizations and study interrelationships between agencies. For instance, do agency structural characteristics affect department-level use of force rates (Smith 2004; Willits and Nowacki 2014)? Why is innovation likely to occur in some departments more than others (Morabito 2008; Skogan and Hartnett 2005; Weisburd and Lum 2005)? In contrast, organizational behavior focuses on the individual within the organizational context, or a micro-level approach (Porter, Lawler, and Hackman 1975). Organizational behavioral researchers examine the informal organization, workgroups, and culture as well as the effects of the organization on individual behavior, values, and attitudes. Do officers accept new reforms (Morabito, Watson, and Draine 2013)? How can the organization encourage officers to engage in certain behaviors (Johnson 2009, 2010; Mastrofski, Ritti, and Snipes 1994).

After successfully proposing the idea of a special issue on police organizations to the *Journal of Crime and Justice's* editor, Mike Leiber, we approached scholars in the field who had done or were doing organizational theory or behavioral research across levels of analysis: the industry, the department, or the individual. The empirical research in this area also covers various units of analysis: states, counties, cities, organizations, census blocks, and within and across individuals. The articles in this special issue provide variation across the level and units of analysis and showcase how theory can be used to explain structures, operations, and behaviors within police organizations. The papers in this issue are organized roughly by the level of analysis from industry to the individual.

The study by Matthew Matusiak, William King, and Edward Maguire focused on how the larger institutional sphere affects police chiefs' priorities in Texas. The authors used institutional theory to explain variation across three agency priorities: preserving law and order, maintaining relationships with constituents, and adopting policy or tactical innovations. Using structural equation modeling to measure the influence of various institutional sectors (e.g., national media, local emergency medical organizations, and police employee associations), they then modeled the impact of those sectors along with controls on the chiefs' priorities. They found support for institutional theory in that 'perceptions of all seven institutional sectors had a significant effect on at least one measure of organizational priorities.' Matusiak et al. strengthened the institutional theory scaffolding that has routinely found industry-level factors do influence policing. While more empirical work must be done to test institutional theory, especially measurement of key concepts, there is a growing consensus among the extant research in support of institutional pressures affecting law enforcement decision-making.

Melissa Morabito, April Pattavina, and Linda Williams used organizational indicators and situational factors to predict arrest and clearance of sexual assault cases in 152 police departments. Specifically, they hypothesized those departments with a workforce more representative of women in the community will have higher arrest and clearance rates for sexual assault cases. Using representational bureaucracy theory, they failed to find support for direct effects for female representativeness, but speculated a tipping point has yet to be reached that would show an effect.

In the study by Thomas Holt, Kristie Blevins, and Ruth Waddell Smith, the work stress and job satisfaction of forensic scientists was considered in light of individual and organizational factors. Their research question was whether scientists working for and in law enforcement agencies feel any undue stress or low satisfaction given the independent nature of scientific work in a more structured criminal justice system. The organizational factors they looked at include overtime, management support, and relationships with prosecutors. Building on research on the stress and satisfaction of law enforcement officers, this study found that an organizational misfit can lead to higher stress, namely working longer hours, having a poor working relationship with a courtroom workgroup, low manager support, and role ambiguity.

Natalie Kroovand Hipple, Edmund McGarrell, Mallory O'Brien, and Beth Huebner examined problem-solving policing at the organizational level across four agencies. Specifically, the authors looked at gun-crime incident reviews in the police departments of Detroit, Indianapolis, Milwaukee, and St. Louis. By examining the incident review process in four separate sites, the authors could understand how organizational-level differences affected the development of the review process.

Michael Kyle and David White looked at police officer buy-in for the use of body-worn cameras. This technical innovation has been rapidly adopted in part because of the current focus on officer-involved shootings of citizens. The authors examined how officers view camera implementation given their perceptions of organizational justice. They hypothesized that the concept of organizational justice (composed of procedural justice, interpersonal justice, and informational justice) will be a strong predictor of officer support for body-worn camera implementation. Specifically, when department leadership explains the need and value of the technology and involves officers in the process, officers may be less fearful of the consequences and trust the organization is considerate of their concerns. Kyle and White found that organizational justice is a significant predictor of positive attitudes toward body-worn camera implementation.

In 'Understanding the culture of craft: Lessons from two police agencies,' James Willis and Stephen Mastrofski revisited the concept of police subculture. Officers in their study rated various aspects of the craft of policing, including views of top performing officers, causes of undesirable results of police-citizen interactions, and perceptions of skill and knowledge in promotion. Based on their findings, the authors argued for a 'more textured assessment of police culture,' specifically on how officers view the various way in which they do their work (or the craft culture). This view diverges from scholarship on policing culture focusing on negative police traits such as machismo, authoritarianism, and cynicism. Their research should direct policy-makers, especially policy derived from scientific best practices, to consider how line officers would view the efficacy of policy from a practical point of view.

The articles in this special issue consider police organizations and their behavior, as well as the behavior of individuals situated within police organizations. The current controversies surrounding policing and police organizations illuminate the importance of scholarship, policies, and practices that address both the individual and the organizational level within the profession. While much attention and discourse has focused on police officers and the decisions they make as individuals (i.e., to use force, to make an arrest, or to grant a citizen's request for service or intervention), it is imperative to recognize that officers are positioned within organizations. Officers act as independent agents, yet they do so within the structure, policies, training, culture, tradition, and context of their employing organizations. While the influence of police organizations on personnel is not infinite, it is also not infinitesimal (Mastrofski and Ritti 1992).

Efforts to enhance, improve, or reform policing need to consider the reciprocal relationship between organizations and individuals. Providing police organizations with improved equipment, for example, is likely to be of limited efficacy if personnel are not trained on the proper use of that equipment and then held accountable for its application within relevant policies and contexts. Providing police officers with training on a new patrolling strategy is unlikely to yield optimal results if requisite changes to staffing and deployment are not also made within the organization. Major efforts to reform policing often focus on modifications to police organizations, while corresponding changes in police personnel and their behaviors are implied but less directly addressed in a prescriptive fashion (i.e., President's Task Force on 21st Century Policing's 2015).

Analogously, policing scholars need to continue to examine organizations, individuals, and their interplay in understanding the behavior and decision-making of each. Community policing represents a prime example of this situation. Studies of police organizations suggested community policing was being commonly adopted in the US during the 1990s (Zhao, Lovrich, and Thurman 1999). Yet studies often found limited evidence as to the penetration of this policing approach and its ability to demonstrate purported outcomes (Zhao, Lovrich, and Robinson 2001). Was the problem the organizations or the individuals? Was the problem giving people enough training and acculturation to win hearts and minds, or was the problem a failure of organizations to change culture, structure, supervision, and organizational practice in the right ways? Were the limitations of community policing a product of an inherently flawed idea, recalcitrant police officers, organizations that failed to recognize the approach required changes at the organizational level, or some combination of these problems?

If the academic and policy-making community wishes to see more advances in the policing profession, police organizations and leaders need to be guided by research that drills deeper into the complex milieu of the interplay between individuals and the organizations within which they are situated. More research into organizations, organizational theory, and the diffusion of innovative practices are key elements of meeting this need. Initiatives intended to advance the profession must be formulated and pursued with a greater understanding of the behavior of organizations and individuals. While the recent decades have born witness to advances in the understanding of police organizations, and while the articles included in this special issue build that base of knowledge, there remains work for the academic community.

Note

1. Although writing contemporaneously, key organizational works by Weber and Fayol would not be translated into English until the mid-twentieth century (Wren 1972).

References

Critchley, T. A. 1967. *A History of Police in England and Wales 900–1966*. London: Constable.

Fayol, H. 1949. *General and Industrial Management*. Translated by C. Storrs. London: Sir Isaac Pitman and Sons.

Gulick, L. 1937. "Notes on the Theory of Organization." In *Papers on the Science of Administration*, edited by L. Gulick, L. Urwick, J. D. Mooney, H. Fayol, H. S. Dennison, L. J. Henderson, and V. A. Graicunas, 1–46. New York: Institute of Public Administration.

Johnson, R. R. 2009. "Explaining Police Officer Drug Activity Through Expectancy Theory." *Policing: An International Journal of Police Strategies & Management* 32 (1): 6–20.

Johnson, R. R. 2010. "Making Domestic Violence Arrests: A Test of Expectancy Theory." *Policing: An International Journal of Police Strategies & Management* 33 (3): 531–547.

Klockars, C. B. 1985. *The Idea of Police*. Beverly Hills, CA: Sage.

Mastrofski, S. D., and R. R. Ritti. 1992. "You Can Lead a Horse to Water: A Case Study of a Police Department's Response to Stricter Drunk-driving Laws." *Justice Quarterly* 9 (3): 465–491.

Mastrofski, S. D., R. R. Ritti, and J. B. Snipes. 1994. "Expectancy Theory and Police Productivity in DUI Enforcement." *Law & Society Review* 28 (1): 113–148.

Morabito, M. S. 2008. "The Adoption of Police Innovation: The Role of the Political Environment." *Policing: An International Journal of Police Strategies & Management* 31 (3): 466–484.

Morabito, M. S., A. Watson, and J. Draine. 2013. "Police Officer Acceptance of New Innovation: The Case of Crisis Intervention Teams." *Policing: An International Journal of Police Strategies & Management* 36 (2): 421–436.

Porter, L. W., E. E. Lawler, and J. R. Hackman. 1975. *Behavior in Organizations*. New York: McGraw-Hill.

President's Task Force on 21st Century Policing. 2015. *Final Report of the President's Task Force on 21st Century Policing*. Washington, DC: Department of Justice, Office of Community Oriented Policing Services.

Scott, W. R., and G. F. Davis. 2007. *Organizations and Organizing: Rational, Natural, and Open System Perspectives*. Upper Saddle River, NJ: Pearson.

Simon, H. A. 1952. "Comments on the Theory of Organizations." *The American Political Science Review* 46 (4): 1130–1139.

Skogan, W. G., and S. M. Hartnett. 2005. "The Diffusion of Information Technology in Policing." *Police Practice and Research: An International Journal* 6 (5): 401–417.

Smith, B. W. 2004. "Structural and Organizational Predictors of Homicide by Police." *Policing: An International Journal of Police Strategies & Management* 27 (4): 539–557.

Starbuck, W. H. 2003. "The Origins of Organization Theory." In *Oxford Handbook of Organization Theory*, edited by H. Tsoukas and C. Knudsen, 143–182. New York: Oxford University Press.

Taylor, F. W. 1913. *The Principles of Scientific Management*. New York: Harper & Brothers.

Tompkins, J. R. 2005. *Organization Theory and Public Management*. Belmont, CA: Wadsworth.

Uchida, C. D. 1997. "The Development of the American Police: An Historical Overview." In *Critical Issues in Policing: Contemporary Readings*, edited by R. G. Dunham and G. P. Alpert, 18–35. Prospect Heights, IL: Waveland.

Weber, M. 1946. *From Max Weber: Essays in Sociology*. Translated by H. H. Gerth and C. W. Mills. New York: Oxford University Press.

Weisburd, D., and C. Lum. 2005. "The Diffusion of Computerized Crime Mapping in Policing: Linking Research and Practice." *Police Practice and Research* 6 (5): 419–434.

Willits, D. W., and J. S. Nowacki. 2014. "Police Organisation and Deadly Force: An Examination of Variation Across Large and Small Cities." *Policing and Society* 24 (1): 63–80.

Wren, D. A. 1972. *The Evolution of Management Thought*. New York: Ronald Press Company.

Zhao, J., N. P. Lovrich, and T. H. Robinson. 2001. "Community Policing: Is it Changing the Basic Functions of Policing? Findings from a Longitudinal Study of 200+ Municipal Police Agencies." *Journal of Criminal Justice* 29 (5): 365–377.

Zhao, J., N. P. Lovrich, and Q. Thurman. 1999. "The Status of Community Policing in American Cities: Facilitators and Impediments Revisited." *Policing: An International Journal of Police Strategies and Management* 22 (1): 7–9.

George W. Burruss

Matthew J. Giblin and Joseph A. Schafer

How perceptions of the institutional environment shape organizational priorities: findings from a survey of police chiefs

Matthew C. Matusiak , William R. King and Edward R. Maguire

ABSTRACT

A long tradition of research has examined the influence of organizational environments on criminal justice agencies. Based on survey data from a sample of local police chiefs, this study explores the effects of the institutional environment on police agency priorities. Specifically, we investigate how the perceived importance of different sectors of the institutional environment influences police agency priorities, as reported by police chiefs. The analyses reveal that certain sectors of the institutional environment exert greater influence on police organizational priorities than others. Moreover, the influence of institutional sectors differs according to the specific type of priority. Our findings reveal that institutional considerations exert more consistent effects on the importance of maintaining relationships with constituents than on maintaining law and order or adopting innovative practices. We draw on institutional theory in explaining the study's findings.

Introduction

Nearly a half-century ago, Wilson (1968) posited that the behavior of local police agencies was influenced by the structure and culture of local politics. Though now dated, Wilson's classic study of police agencies in eight cities remains one of the most influential academic works in criminal justice (Maguire and Uchida 2000; Zhao, He, and Lovrich 2006, Zhao, Ren, and Lovrich 2010) and has inspired numerous empirical tests (e.g., Crank 1990; Hassell, Zhao, and Maguire 2003; Langworthy 1985; Liederbach and Travis 2008; Matusiak 2014; Slovak 1986). Wilson's study was published at a pivotal time in the development of two bodies of research and theory, one focusing on complex organizations and the other on criminal justice. Within the former, older closed-systems models of organizations were being replaced by an open-systems perspective that acknowledged the powerful influence of the environment in which organizations are situated (Lawrence and Lorsch 1967; Thompson 1967). Scholars married this new open-systems perspective on organizations with the growing academic interest in the structures and behaviors of police and other criminal justice agencies (e.g., Clark, Hall, and Hutchinson 1977; Reiss, Jr. and Bordua 1967). Wilson's study served as the catalyst for generations of subsequent research focused on explaining interagency variations in policing from a variety of theoretical perspectives (e.g., Katz 1997; Katz, Maguire, and Roncek 2002; Langworthy 1985; Matusiak 2013; Smith and Holmes 2003; Stucky 2005; Zhao 1994).

One of the most fruitful areas of research to emerge from the open-systems perspective has been the study of how police organizations are influenced by their institutional environments. As Crank and Langworthy (1992, 341) note, policing occurs 'in an environment saturated with institutional values.' The institutional environment is home to a variety of entities with the ability to influence the well-being of police organizations. Crank and Langworthy (1992, 342) emphasize that police agencies derive legitimacy by conforming to 'institutional expectations of what the appropriate structures and activities for a police department are.' The study of this aspect of organizational environments is based on institutional theory, which stems from the pioneering work of Meyer and Rowan (1977), DiMaggio and Powell (1983), and other notable organizational scholars. Institutional theory has had a profound influence on organizational scholarship across multiple disciplines. A growing body of scholarship has applied this perspective to understanding the impact of the institutional environment on police organizations (Crank 2003; Crank and Langworthy 1992, 1996; Giblin 2006; Giblin and Burruss 2009; Giblin, Schafer, and Burruss 2009; Katz 2001; Matusiak 2013).

The present study builds on previous applications of institutional theory to the study of police organizations by testing the influence of police chiefs' perceptions of the institutional environment on agency priorities. We focus on seven sectors of the institutional environment: federal and state law enforcement agencies, national media, local media, police officer associations, elected officials, other criminal justice agencies, and emergency medical service providers. Drawing on survey data from a sample of police chiefs, we estimate a structural equation model that links perceptions of the institutional environment with agency priorities. We begin by providing a brief overview of institutional theory in the study of organizations. We review previous scholarship that has applied institutional theory to the study of policing. Then, we present our data, methods, findings, and conclusions.

Literature review

Institutional theory

According to institutional theory, organizations are heavily influenced by the institutional environments in which they are embedded (Donaldson 1995). The institutional environment for police agencies is comprised of various elements that establish norms and expectations about what a good police agency should look like. Powerful entities in the institutional environment – sometimes referred to as institutional sovereigns – can exert considerable influence over the structures and operations of police organizations. Sovereigns may be local, state, national, or international. They include police professional organizations (such as the International Association of Chiefs of Police), state and national accreditation bodies, state training and certification boards, other criminal justice agencies, and organizations responsible for related functions, such as emergency response. Sovereigns may also include elected officials, the media, community groups, and special interest groups. These entities are important because they are able to confer or withhold legitimacy. Thus, a key aspect of being a skilled leader is learning how to navigate the institutional environment and satisfy the demands of numerous constituencies to preserve legitimacy.

Legitimacy provides an organization with numerous benefits. According to Maguire (2014):

> [L]egitimacy helps to establish autonomy, generate additional political and civic support, and maximize the flow of resources. This primal concern with legitimacy also leads police agencies to adopt policies, practices, and structures considered *de rigueur* in the policing industry. These features may not suit their unique contexts or needs; yet adopting them enables the agency to appear progressive. (87–88)

Organizations in highly institutionalized environments acquire legitimacy by adopting certain signs and symbols of technical proficiency – such as having the right types of programs, policies, or special units – rather than by providing any actual evidence that these structural or operational elements improve performance. This preoccupation with the appearance of being progressive explains, for instance, how a police agency that is not facing a serious gang problem might end up establishing a specialized gang unit (Katz 2001). Legitimacy is built through an interactive process between organizations and their environments (Aldrich 1999; Donaldson 1995). Organizations that are most responsive and most adept at meeting the expectations of their institutional environments (for example, by changing their structure in ways widely believed to be socially acceptable) are granted greater legitimacy and are therefore more likely to gain access to crucial resources. On the other hand, organizations that are deemed unresponsive to their environments may be 'more vulnerable to claims that they are negligent, irrational, or unnecessary' (Meyer and Rowan 1977, 349).

Institutional environments are complex and may give rise to competing demands on organizations. Moreover, demands from the institutional environment often conflict with those arising out of concerns with technical proficiency. As a result, organizations in heavily institutionalized environments must find a way to address a mix of competing institutional and technical demands in order to preserve legitimacy, effectiveness, and efficiency. One way organizations can resolve this conflict is by decoupling visible policies and structures from routine operating practices (Meyer and Rowan 1977). In this way, organizations can buffer their technical core (where the majority of the organization's work gets done) from external pressures imposed by the environment (Thompson 1967). Decoupling enables the core work of the organization to continue undisturbed while more peripheral elements of the organization generate the appearance of being responsive to demands from the institutional environment. The decoupling phenomenon helps explain why so much of what passes as police reform is really just 'symbolic reform at the edges' (Maguire, Uchida, and Hassell 2015, 90).[1]

Institutional theory in policing

Policing scholars have embraced institutional theory despite formidable challenges in the operationalization and measurement of key concepts (Maguire 2014). Building upon Crank and Langworthy's (1992) initial application of institutional theory to the police, researchers have explored how police agencies seek to establish legitimacy by adapting to the expectations of key actors or entities in their institutional environments. For example, studies have reported on the legitimacy implications of agencies adopting – or failing to adopt – community-oriented policing (Maguire and Katz 2002; Zhao, Lovrich, and Robinson 2001), Compstat (Willis 2011; Willis and Mastrofski 2011; Willis, Mastrofski, and Weisburd 2007), green policing (Worrall 2010), special units (Katz 2001), and a variety of other phenomena. Overall, police agencies seem to benefit when they adopt innovations that are viewed favorably within certain influential sectors of their institutional environments. Other researchers have addressed the importance of stakeholder perceptions (Maguire and King 2007; Vitale 2005) in determining legitimacy. Responding to public sentiment demonstrates to powerful outside constituents that police organizations are responsive to their concerns (Crank 2003). At the same time, police agencies that are not responsive to concerns or expectations arising from their institutional environments may end up paying a hefty price in terms of lost legitimacy or resources. Taken to the extreme, legitimacy crises can ultimately lead to the disbanding of a police agency, especially for smaller agencies (King 2014).

During the 1990s, police departments in the USA came under considerable pressure to adopt community policing. Many responded by establishing specialized community policing units or positions that left the core work of the agency to continue policing as usual. This enabled police leaders to report that they were doing community policing, thus satisfying demands from their institutional environment without disrupting routine operating practices (Maguire 1997; Zhao, Lovrich, and Robinson 2001). Research on the adoption of community policing in American police departments is consistent with propositions from institutional theory. For instance, some research suggests that police agencies may have claimed to practice community policing to enhance their eligibility for federal funding (Maguire and Katz 2002; Maguire and Mastrofski 2000). According to Crank (1994), community policing emerged largely out of concerns with police legitimacy. He argues that community policing resulted from two myths. The first was the myth that communities are comprised of like-minded individuals who share similar histories and perceptions and have similar expectations of police. The second was the historically romanticized myth of police officers as watchmen who look out for their community's best interests.

Taken together, these myths served as the basis for community policing and provided a legitimating mechanism that enabled police organizations to 'ceremonially regain the legitimacy' they lost in the 1960s (Crank 1994, 347).

Researchers have also applied institutional theory to the widespread diffusion of the Compstat model (Willis 2011; Willis and Mastrofski 2011; Willis, Mastrofski, and Weisburd 2007). Compstat and similar initiatives are a source of legitimacy for police organizations because they demonstrate that police are doing the 'right things' to control crime. Willis, Mastrofski, and Weisburd (2007) found that in the three agencies they studied, the implementation of Compstat was motivated by the need for the organization to appear more progressive to its constituents, not by a genuine desire to improve performance. Willis and Mastrofski (2011, 86) note that:

> [T]he display of crime statistics and electronic maps at regular Compstat accountability meetings sent a powerful message that the organization was taking crime seriously whether or not these data had a significant influence on the selection of effective crime prevention strategies.

Incorporating new technologies often allows police agencies to demonstrate that they are being responsive to demands from the environment, whether or not such changes improve technical proficiency.

The application of institutional theory to the study of policing has also focused on the process of organizational change. When organizations implement changes in response to pressures or demands from the institutional environment, they are said to become more 'isomorphic' (consistent or concordant) with their environment. Institutional theorists argue that isomorphic pressures tend to take three primary forms: coercive, mimetic, and normative (DiMaggio and Powell 1983). Coercive isomorphism occurs when an organization is forced through legal or contractual obligations to make certain changes. For instance, courts may order police agencies to adopt certain changes to protect people's civil liberties. Mimetic isomorphism occurs when an organization copies or mimics the structures or practices of other organizations. Previous research has demonstrated the importance that police officials attribute to the practices of other police organizations (Giblin 2006; Matusiak 2013). Finally, normative isomorphism occurs as a result of the diffusion of norms and standards throughout an organizational field. It is a process of homogenization that results from shared cultural understandings within an organizational field (such as within the policing field) about which structures and practices are most appropriate, regardless of whether there is evidence to support these beliefs (DiMaggio and Powell 1983).

Some scholars have considered the impact of the institutional environment on the diffusion of innovation among police agencies. For instance, Roberts and Roberts, Jr. (2009) found that police departments were more likely to incorporate the use of computers for crime mapping if they had contact with people in other departments employing the same technologies. Similarly, Giblin (2006) investigated the role of institutional isomorphism in the diffusion of crime analysis units. While he did not find *quantitative* evidence of mimetic isomorphism in organizational structures, *qualitative* evidence revealed that police agencies tend to emulate their peers with regard to crime analysis activities and practices, but not with regard to 'the structure of the crime analysis function' (Giblin 2006, 660). Funding and crime rates were largely irrelevant, but accreditation had a marginally significant impact on the creation of crime analysis units (Giblin 2006). These findings suggest that crime analysis units may have been established, in part, in response to legitimacy concerns. Police organizations are more likely to adopt innovations when the innovations are supported by the institutional environment (Burruss and Giblin 2014).

Institutional theory presents a variety of challenges for empirical research, not the least of which is difficulty in operationalizing many of its key concepts. Various scholars have emphasized the need for empirical tests of institutional theory (Katz, Maguire, and Roncek 2002; Maguire and Uchida 2000; Willis, Mastrofski, and Weisburd 2007). For instance, Willis, Mastrofski, and Weisburd (2007, 153) conclude that while the literature 'offers an intriguing and provocative perspective of the structures and practices of policing, it does not offer thorough and conclusive empirical tests of the superiority of institutional theory.' The present study seeks to contribute to this body of research by examining how police chiefs perceive various sectors of their institutional environments and how these perceptions shape agency priorities.

While existing research has documented numerous examples of institutional environments influencing the structures and operations of police agencies (Burruss and Giblin 2014; Giblin 2006; Hassell, Zhao, and Maguire 2003; Katz 2001; Roberts and Roberts, Jr. 2009; Willis and Mastrofski 2011; Zhao, Lovrich, and Robinson 2001), the precise conduits through which these effects are transmitted are not yet well understood. By what process, exactly, does the institutional environment influence the goals, structures, and behaviors of police organizations? Police chiefs serve as the principal boundary spanners in police agencies, holding a unique and crucial position at the intersection of the organization and its environment. Researchers have highlighted the crucial role of police chiefs:

> A police chief is the instrumental actor at the nexus of police tradition and antagonistic external interests. More or less influential individually, the chief is, in any case, a reference point for organizing the complex processes by which the principles of police legitimacy and modes of their expression are socially constructed. (Hunt and Magenau 1993, 84)

Despite widespread acknowledgment of the importance of police chiefs as boundary spanners between police agencies and their environments, little is known about how they perceive their institutional environments or how they weigh the relative influence of various environmental sectors. In this paper, we explore the proposition that different sectors of the institutional environment may exert differential impacts on agency priorities as reported by chiefs. We draw primarily on research and theory on the relationships between organizations and their institutional environments to frame our approach.

Much has been written about police chiefs in general, as well as their likely prospects for effecting change and being good leaders (Schafer 2013). Rather than viewing police chiefs as omnipotent leaders who have a free hand to run their organizations as they see fit, researchers emphasize the considerable constraints that chiefs face in their efforts to alter the status quo in police organizations. For instance, Mastrofski (1998, 183) notes that the job of a police chief, particularly in large urban departments, is not so different from a rodeo cowboy 'who with great skill manages merely to stay astride his bucking bronco until the bell sounds.' Little, however, has been written about how chiefs perceive the institutional environment and how these perceptions shape their decisions and behaviors. We contend that the influences exerted by the institutional environment on police agency priorities operate primarily through police chiefs. Put differently, police chiefs represent a central conduit through which institutional environments exert influence over police agencies. Testing the association between police chiefs' perceptions of the institutional environment and the priorities of police agencies provides a partial test of the extent to which institutional environments influence police organizations.

Data and methods

Data for the current study were drawn from a survey of police chiefs who participated in the Texas Police Chiefs Leadership Series (TPCLS) program. The TPCLS is mandated by the State of Texas, which requires that chiefs from all local and special law enforcement agencies participate in 40 hours of continuing education every 2 years. The TPCLS is administered by the Law Enforcement Management Institute of Texas, which is located in Huntsville. Participating chiefs completed self-administered, paper surveys between October 2011 and July 2013. Surveys were administered to 994 participants, with 926 chiefs providing completed surveys (a 93.2% response rate). Fourteen of these respondents were later deemed ineligible based on our selection criteria, leaving 912 useable survey responses from 898 unique police agencies.[2]

Data from the 2008 Census of State and Local Law Enforcement Agencies (CSLLEA) indicate that there are approximately 1913 law enforcement agencies in Texas. However, the TPCLS does not service all of these agencies. Constable/marshal agencies ($n = 605$) and county sheriffs' departments ($n = 254$) are not included in TPCLS programs because they are led by elected officials, which makes them unique relative to police chiefs, who are typically appointed, not elected (Falcone and Wells 1995). Additionally, chiefs in major cities (population greater than 100,000) ($n = 32$) participate in a special continuing education program separate from the TPCLS that is directed specifically toward issues affecting larger municipalities. Therefore, of the approximately 1022 remaining agencies whose chiefs are mandated to participate in the TPCLS, our survey was administered to 977 (95.6%) of them. We collected useable data from 898 unique agencies (87.9% of the eligible agencies in Texas).

The survey gathered data on three types of variables useful for understanding the relationships between police chiefs and their institutional environments. First, the survey asked police chiefs to rate the importance of a variety of agency functions. We treated the responses to these survey items as indicators of the organization's priorities. Based on these indicators, we computed three composite measures of organizational priorities that serve as the *dependent* variables in this study. Second, the survey asked police chiefs to rate the potential influence of a variety of entities (such as elected officials and local media outlets) located in different sectors of the institutional environment. Measures of the perceived influence of seven sectors of the institutional environment serve as the key *independent* variables in this study. Third, demographic characteristics of police chiefs (such as age, education, and tenure), and basic descriptive information about the police agency (e.g., agency size) serve as control variables in this study.

Dependent variables

The dependent variables in this study are three composite measures of organizational priorities constructed from 13 survey items using confirmatory factor analysis (CFA). These composites are intended to measure three different dimensions of organizational priorities: maintaining law and order, maintaining positive working relationships with constituents, and adopting innovations. For each of the 13 items, police chiefs were asked to rate the importance of agency priorities on an ordinal scale ranging from 0 (not important at all) to 5 (extremely important). The 13 survey items are listed in Table 1 along with the dimensions they are intended to measure and the factor loadings for each item. Factor loadings ranged from a low .66 to a high of .93, with a mean of .80. The model fit the data well according to multiple criteria.[3] The three composite measures have strong positive correlations with one another (ranging from .50 to .71), but the correlations are not large enough to raise concerns about discriminant validity.[4]

Independent variables

The main independent variables of interest in this study are composite measures rating the influence of seven sectors of the institutional environment. Each measure is an unweighted additive index comprised of multiple survey items with ordinal response options. The seven sectors include federal/state law enforcement (6 items), national media (4 items), local media (2 items), police employee associations (4 items), elected officials (3 items), local criminal justice organizations (5 items), and local

Table 1. Confirmatory factor analysis results for three measures of organizational priorities.

Indicators	Loadings
Maintain law and order	
Enforce laws and local ordinances	0.660
Control or have low rates of violent crime	0.897
Control or have low rates of nonviolent crime	0.916
Maintain order	0.786
Maintain relationships with constituents	
Ensure that police employees are satisfied with their jobs	0.710
Keep the agency running smoothly – everyone should get along	0.695
Maintain a good working relationship with my officers and employees	0.719
Have a positive image in the local media	0.864
Have positive relationships with local politicians	0.791
Have positive relationships with local residents	0.806
Adopt innovations	
Adopt innovations/programs/tactics other agencies have adopted	0.913
Adopt innovations/programs/tactics publicized by state or federal agencies	0.927
Adopt innovations/programs/tactics because they can be funded by grant money	0.749

emergency response organizations (2 items). Each item required police chiefs to rank the potential influence, whether positive or negative, of a particular constituency. Participating chiefs ranked each constituency on an ordinal scale ranging from 0 (not important at all) to 5 (extreme importance). The survey items used to measure the perceived importance of each sector are listed in Appendix 1.[5]

In addition to the independent variables included in the model for substantive purposes, we also controlled for the influence of a variety of individual-level and agency-level characteristics of the respondents. We included five individual-level characteristics of the respondents as independent variables in the model: sex, race, education, years of experience in law enforcement, and whether the chief was hired from inside or outside the agency. For purposes of this study, sex (female = 0, male = 1) and race (nonwhite = 0, white = 1) were both treated as binary variables. Participants were primarily male (96.7%) and the majority of participants were white (79.0%). Education is an ordinal variable that ranges from 1 (high school diploma or GED) to 7 (PhD).[6] More than half (57.4%) of the respondents reported having an Associate's degree or beyond. Years of experience in law enforcement is a continuous variable that ranges from 1 to 47 years, with a mean of 26 years. Whether the chief was hired from inside or outside the agency is a binary variable (external = 0, internal = 1). More than half of the participating chiefs (54.9%) were hired for their current position from outside of the agency.

We also included three independent variables to control for jurisdictional/agency characteristics. Two dummy variables were included in the model to control for the nature of the jurisdiction (urban, suburban, or rural): one for whether the department serves an urban jurisdiction (no = 0, yes = 1) and one for whether the department serves a rural jurisdiction (no = 0, yes = 1). In both cases, suburban agencies serve as the reference category. Approximately 40.5% of chiefs reported that their agencies serve rural communities, with 26.5% serving suburban areas and 33% serving urban areas. Finally, we included a measure of agency size based on the number of full-time sworn officers with arrest powers. Agency size is a continuous variable that ranges from 0 to 474, with a mean of approximately 20 and a median of 9 full-time sworn officers.[7]

Results

We estimated a single structural equation model to test the effects of the independent variables on the dependent variables. The model included three dependent variables measuring organizational priorities as articulated by participating police chiefs, and 15 independent variables (7 measuring the respondent's assessment of the importance of different sectors of the institutional environment, 5 measuring individual-level characteristics of respondents, and 3 measuring agency/jurisdictional characteristics). Because the three dependent variables are specified as latent variables, the model includes both a measurement (CFA) component and a structural (regression) component. The whole model was estimated simultaneously using a robust mean and variance-adjusted weighted least squares estimator in Mplus (Muthén and Muthén 1998–2012). The model fit the data well according to several fit measures (χ^2 = 727.03, df = 265, p < .000; RMSEA = .046; CFI = .973; TLI = 0.964; WRMR = 1.17).[8] Table 2 contains standardized linear regression coefficients and associated p-values for the structural portion of the model.[9]

Taken together, the independent variables in the model explained 24.5% of the variation in police chiefs' ratings of the importance of *maintaining law and order*. Three of the seven institutional sectors (local media, local criminal justice organizations, and local emergency medical organizations) exerted a statistically significant effect on ratings of the importance of maintaining law and order. Three of the control variables (sex, race, and education) also exerted significant effects on these ratings. Respondents who were male, white, and more educated were *less* likely to view maintaining law and order as important.

The independent variables explained 33.1% of the variation in police chiefs' ratings of the importance of *maintaining relationships with constituents*. Six of the seven institutional sectors (all but federal/state law enforcement agencies) exerted statistically significant effects on ratings of the importance of maintaining relationships with constituents. Two of the control variables (race and education) also exerted

Table 2. Linear regression results.

	DV1: Maintain law & order		DV2: Maintain relationships		DV3: Adopt innovations	
	β	p	β	p	β	p
Institutional sectors						
Federal/state law enforcement	.088	.082	.025	.638	.309	**.000**
National media	−.040	.371	−.096	**.031**	−.040	.331
Local media	.103	**.007**	.077	**.034**	.031	.355
Police employee associations	.072	.080	.220	**.000**	.224	**.000**
Elected officials	−.002	.957	.108	**.005**	−.026	.455
Local criminal justice organizations	.241	**.000**	.204	**.000**	−.002	.966
Local emergency medical organizations	.091	**.022**	.100	**.014**	.164	**.000**
Controls (individual-level)						
Years in law enforcement	−.034	.419	.024	.569	−.030	.427
Sex (male = 1)	−.129	**.007**	−.069	.093	−.103	**.002**
Race (white = 1)	−.109	**.010**	−.189	**.000**	−.294	**.000**
Education	−.148	**.001**	−.203	**.000**	−.110	**.009**
Hired from inside (yes = 1)	−.007	.872	−.032	.457	−.016	.680
Controls (agency-level)						
Urban jurisdiction (yes = 1)	.058	.232	.082	.105	.033	.455
Rural jurisdiction (yes = 1)	.010	.849	.004	.931	−.002	.956
Agency size (full-time sworn)	.044	.396	−.023	.629	.036	.419
Explained variance (R^2, %)	24.5		33.1		37.6	

Notes: Model fit statistics: $\chi^2 = 727.03$, df = 265, $p < .000$; RMSEA = .046; CFI = .973; TLI = 0.964; WRMR = 1.17. Bold values represent statistically significant relationships.

significant effects on these ratings. White respondents and those who were more educated were *less* likely than others to view maintaining relationships with constituents as important.

Taken together, the independent variables explained 37.6% of the variation in police chiefs' ratings of the importance of *adopting innovations*. Three of the seven institutional sectors (federal/state law enforcement, police employee associations, and local emergency medical organizations) exerted a statistically significant effect on ratings of the importance of adopting innovations. Three of the control variables (sex, race, and education) also exerted significant effects on these ratings. Respondents who were male, white, and more educated were *less* likely to view adopting innovations as important.

Discussion

All organizations are embedded in environments with which they must interact regularly. For most organizations, the environment is not a homogeneous entity. Instead, it is complex, dynamic, and in some cases, turbulent. Moreover, the environment is not merely a source of clients, raw materials, funding, and other tangible resources; it is also a source of legitimacy. Certain types of organizations, like police departments, operate in highly institutionalized environments that exert considerable pressure on them to adopt certain structures, policies, or practices. These pressures do not result from 'technological or material imperatives, but rather from cultural norms, symbols, beliefs, and rituals' (Suchman 1995, 571). In such environments, organizations that are responsive to these institutional pressures acquire legitimacy and enhance their prospects for survival 'independent of the immediate efficacy of the acquired practices and procedures' (Meyer and Rowan 1977, 340).

Due to the powerful influence of institutional environments on organizations, wise leaders scan the environment for information that may be useful for the organization's well-being. Environments vary in complexity but are typically comprised of various sectors. The greater the degree of uncertainty within and across these sectors, the greater the intensity of environmental scanning (Choo 2002). As a result of these scanning activities, leaders are able to incorporate information from the environment into the organization's goals, priorities, and other elements. As noted more than a half-century ago by

Thompson and McEwen (1958, 23), determining organizational priorities is a matter of 'defining desired relationships between an organization and its environment.'

In the present study, we focused on the effects of police chiefs' perceptions of the influence of seven environmental sectors on three measures of organizational priorities. Of the 21 resulting regression coefficients, 12 were statistically significant.[10] Perceptions of all seven institutional sectors had a significant effect on at least one measure of organizational priorities. Taken together, these findings suggest that perceptions of the environment may play a role in shaping organizational priorities as reported by police chiefs. Several of the control variables also exerted significant effects on organizational priorities. For instance, police chief race and education were significant in all three models; white chiefs and those who are more educated rated all three agency priorities as less important than nonwhite chiefs and those who are less educated. Female chiefs gave significantly higher ratings to two of the three agency priorities (maintaining law and order and adopting innovations) than male chiefs. Finally, agency size and urbanization were unrelated to all three organizational priorities.

Our findings suggest that police chiefs' assessments of the potential influence of their external environments have an effect on agency priorities. When police chiefs perceive certain environmental sectors as influential, including local media, local criminal justice organizations, and local emergency medical organizations, they are more likely to prioritize the traditional core functions of policing such as law enforcement, crime control, and order maintenance. This finding is consistent with Wilson's (1968) research on local political culture and police agency adaptation. It also highlights the relative lack of influence of other sectors of the environment (such as federal and state law enforcement, the national media, police unions, and politicians) on the extent to which police chiefs prioritize traditional policing functions.

Although only three of the seven environmental sectors had a significant influence on the importance that police chiefs attached to maintaining law and order, six sectors had a significant influence on the importance attached to maintaining positive interactions with constituents. According to institutional theory, legitimacy derives from many sources. For leaders, maintaining legitimacy means routinely interacting with a wide variety of constituents and forming positive relationships with those who are perceived to be influential. These relationship maintenance activities help establish goodwill and prevent misunderstandings or antagonism that could threaten the survival or well-being of the agency. Maintaining positive interactions with constituents is quintessential leadership behavior for those leaders who understand and appreciate the importance of the institutional environment. The only environmental sector that did not influence the importance attached to maintaining positive interactions with constituents was federal and state law enforcement agencies. One possibility for this finding is that among the chiefs of the mostly small police agencies in our sample, federal and state law enforcement agencies may not be particularly salient in their day-to-day work, especially in comparison with key *local* stakeholders.

Three of the seven environmental sectors – federal/state law enforcement agencies, police employee associations, and local emergency medical organizations – had a significant influence on the importance police chiefs attached to adopting innovations. Little is known about the specific role of various sectors of the environment in promoting or inhibiting the adoption of innovation in police agencies. The measures of innovation adoption used in this study focus primarily on those that are copied or diffused from other agencies or funded through external grants. These mechanisms for diffusing innovation are inherently institutional in nature. Future research should seek to clarify the precise causal pathways through which these institutional mechanisms penetrate police organizations and promote the adoption of innovation. Qualitative research would seem to be especially helpful for documenting these linkages between police agencies and their environments.

Qualitative research methods may be particularly helpful for understanding the extent to which institutional processes lead organizations within a particular field to become increasingly homogeneous 'in structure, culture, and output' as hypothesized by DiMaggio and Powell (1983, 147). The fact that we observed cross-sectional heterogeneity across agencies with regard to organizational priorities does not allow us to draw direct inferences about the nature or extent of these homogenization processes.

The presence of significant variation within an organizational field means that if agencies are becoming more homogeneous, the process is not yet complete. However, homogenization is a temporal process that should be studied using longitudinal methods, whether quantitative, qualitative, or some combination of the two.

While findings from our analysis of cross-sectional data do not allow for direct inferences about these temporal processes, they do reveal that different sectors of the organizational environment may exert different pressures on police agencies. For instance, it is possible that police agencies, as public organizations, must react to demands from multiple competing institutional environments. They may face pressure to address the immediate needs of various sectors of the local institutional environment while also maintaining legitimacy within the broader regulatory environment of policing (Scott 2008). Police leaders may not only need to contend with a singular institutional environment; they may be faced with competing demands from an overlapping multitude of institutional environments (Scott 1987). The findings of our current research highlight the importance of the local environment surrounding police organizations. However, further research using a variety of methodologies is necessary to parse out the effects of institutional environmental sectors upon police agencies.

Though not directly related to the theoretical issues motivating this paper, our findings with regard to agency size are also noteworthy. Agency size did not have a significant effect on any of the dependent variables in this study. This is an intriguing finding, given that most studies of organizations, whether police agencies or other types of organizations, find that size exerts a powerful influence on a wide variety of organizational characteristics. The agencies in our sample are relatively small, especially when compared with those included in other studies of police agencies. Most quantitative research on police organizations uses data from agencies with 100 or more full-time sworn officers (Matusiak, Campbell, and King 2014). The agencies included in the present study are considerably smaller, with a mean of 20 and a median of 9 full-time sworn officers. The effects of agency size on organizational characteristics may be nonlinear, such that size effects may be more readily observable within certain size ranges. If the effects of agency size are nonlinear, studies like ours that are based primarily on samples of small agencies may not detect size effects.

There are strong reasons to suspect that these differences in size across studies may also be important from a theoretical perspective. For instance, King (2014, 686–687) argued that small police agencies may lack sufficient buffers to protect the agency from intrusion by external constituents. Larger agencies can respond to demands from the institutional environment by establishing symbolic structures such as special units that serve as powerful signals to constituents that the agency is taking their concerns seriously (Katz 1997, 2001). Smaller agencies may not have sufficient slack resources to adopt these types of symbolic responses, therefore they may be more vulnerable to legitimacy crises arising from the external environment. The present findings suggest that police chiefs in smaller agencies are aware of the various sectors in their external environments and that these perceptions influence agency priorities. It is unclear whether these same relationships would persist within a sample of larger agencies.

There are several limitations associated with the current research. First, although the sample represents almost 90% of municipal police agencies in Texas, it is not representative of all police agencies in the USA. Despite this limitation, we cannot think of any compelling reason why the patterns observed in this study would be unique to Texas. Nonetheless, future research should draw on a wider sample of police organizations that is representative of all geographic regions of the USA. The current sample of police chiefs also exhibits a lack of gender and racial diversities. Although female chiefs rated two of the three agency priorities significantly more highly than their male counterparts, female chiefs were a clear minority among Texas chiefs. Overall, research has demonstrated that females make up a small proportion of law enforcement chief executives (Schulz 2003). Future research should seek to clarify the differences between male and female police chiefs with regard to decision-making, leadership styles, and other phenomena. Finally, while the current research is useful for delineating which environmental sectors are perceived by police chiefs as most and least influential, it is unable to explain *why* these perceptions exist. For instance, the data used here do not make it clear what specific demands are placed on police leaders from different environmental sectors. Our findings suggest that chiefs rate certain environmental sectors as more influential than others, but we do not know why. Qualitative methods may be especially useful for clarifying these issues.

Conclusion

Police chiefs, as boundary spanners between their agency and its environment, must be attuned to demands from key constituencies with the power to influence organizational legitimacy. Institutional theory suggests that the most successful boundary spanners are those who routinely scan the environment and are responsive to its cues (Choo 2002). Attending carefully to the needs of the various constituencies in the external environment can help preserve the agency's resources and minimize the extent to which it is targeted by those seeking to criticize, undermine, or otherwise harm it. The present study contributes to a growing body of research on the various mechanisms through which the institutional environment influences police agencies and those who lead them.

Notes

1. Drawing on institutional theory, several researchers have applied the concept of 'loose coupling' to police organizations (see Burruss and Giblin 2014; Crank and Langworthy 1996; Maguire and Katz 2002; Mastrofski, Ritti, and Hoffmaster 1987; Zhao, Lovrich, and Robinson 2001).
2. For purposes of this study, the population of eligible participants included current police chiefs in jurisdictions meeting the TPCLS selection criteria. Among the 14 respondents deemed ineligible for inclusion in the present study, 9 were retired chiefs and 5 were chiefs in major cities when they completed the survey. This left 912 useable responses. Due to leadership transitions in some agencies during the time period covered by the study, more than one chief from the same agency may have participated in the training and completed a survey. As a result, the 912 useable survey responses represent 898 unique agencies.
3. We estimated a measurement model containing only the three latent dependent variables and their indicators. The model fit the data well according to several fit measures (χ^2 = 279.4, df = 59, p < .000; root mean square error of approximation [RMSEA] = .064; confirmatory fit index [CFI] = .987; Tucker-Lewis Index [TLI] = 0.983; WRMR = 1.08). Model estimation and model fit issues are discussed in more detail later in the paper.
4. The zero-order correlations between latent variables are as follows: maintaining relationships and adopting innovation (r = .68); adopting innovation and law/order (r = .50); law/order and maintaining relationships (r = .71).
5. Most composite measures in the social sciences are based on the assumption that the indicators are effects of the underlying latent variable being measured. The logic underlying factor analysis and various measures of reliability is that items sharing a common cause (the latent variable) should be highly correlated with one another. This approach is known as 'reflective' measurement because the items are said to *reflect* the underlying concept being measured. However, in some cases, the latent variable is thought to be caused by the items rather than the other way around. This approach is known as 'formative' measurement because the items are said to *form* the underlying concept being measured. In such instances, conventional approaches to measurement such as factor analysis and internal consistency tests no longer make sense because they are based on the assumption that the items share a common cause. Here, we assume that assessments of the importance of each individual constituency can be combined to form composite measures of the importance of seven sectors of the environment. We do not report measures of reliability because these constructs are based on formative rather than reflective logic (Bollen 2002; Bollen and Lennox 1991). We rely on additive indices because the specification of formative models in a CFA framework raises a number of complex challenges associated with model identification and multicollinearity (Diamantopoulos, Riefler, and Roth 2008).
6. We tested alternative coding schemes for education, including both binary and ordinal specifications. The ordinal response format provided the best fit.
7. Agencies reporting zero full-time sworn officers employed one or more *part-time* sworn officers.
8. Though it is standard to report χ^2 in structural equation models, its diagnostic value as a fit statistic has been questioned because it is often too strict (Bowen and Guo 2012). For the RMSEA, values ranging from .01 to .06 constitute close fit (Browne and Cudeck 1993; Hu and Bentler 1999). For the CFI and the TLI, values of .95 or greater indicate close fit (Hu and Bentler 1999). For WRMR, simulation evidence suggests that values below 1 are indicative of good fit (Yu 2002). Here, the model fits the data well according to CFI, TLI, and RMSEA, but the WRMR is slightly inflated.

9. We computed variance inflation factors (VIFs) for every independent variable to test for collinearity. Only two VIFs exceeded 2 and none exceeded 3, suggesting that collinearity was not problematic in this analysis (see Belsley, Kuh, and Welsch 1980).
10. The regression analysis resulted in 45 coefficients, 21 of which were associated with variables measuring police chiefs' perceptions of the 7 environmental sectors and 24 of which were associated with the control variables included in the model.

Disclosure statement

No potential conflict of interest was reported by the authors.

References

Aldrich, H. 1999. *Organizations Evolving*. London: Sage.
Belsley, D. A., E. Kuh, and R. E. Welsch. 1980. *Regression Diagnostics: Identifying Influential Data and Sources of Collinearity*. New York: Wiley.
Bollen, K. A. 2002. "Latent Variables in Psychology and the Social Sciences." *Annual Review of Psychology* 53: 605–634.
Bollen, K. A., and R. Lennox. 1991. "Conventional Wisdom on Measurement: A Structural Equation Perspective." *Psychological Bulletin* 110 (2): 305–314.
Bowen, N. K., and S. Guo. 2012. *Structural Equation Modeling*. New York: Oxford University Press.
Browne, M., and R. Cudeck. 1993. "Alternative Ways of Assessing Model Fit." In *Testing Structural Equation Models*, edited by K. A. Bollen and J. S. Long, 136–162. Newbury Park, CA: Sage.
Burruss, G. W., and M. J. Giblin. 2014. "Modeling Isomorphism on Policing Innovation: The Role of Institutional Pressures in Adopting Community-Oriented Policing." *Crime and Delinquency* 60 (3): 331–355.
Choo, C. W. 2002. *Environmental Scanning as Information Seeking and Organizational Knowing*. *PrimaVera* Working Paper #2002-01. Amsterdam: University of Amsterdam, Department of Business Studies.
Clark, J. P., R. H. Hall, and B. Hutchinson. 1977. "Interorganizational Relationships and Network Properties as Contextual Variables in the Study of Police Performance." In *Police and Society*, edited by D. H. Bayley, 177–193. Beverly Hills, CA: Sage.
Crank, J. P. 1990. "The Influence of Environmental and Organizational Factors on Police Style in Urban and Rural Environments." *Journal of Research in Crime and Delinquency* 27 (2): 166–189.
Crank, J. P. 1994. "Watchman and Community: Myth and Institutionalization in Policing." *Law and Society Review* 28 (2): 325–352.
Crank, J. P. 2003. "Institutional Theory of Police: A Review of the State of the Art." *Policing: An International Journal of Police Strategies and Management* 26 (2): 186–207.
Crank, J. P., and R. Langworthy. 1992. "An Institutional Perspective of Policing." *The Journal of Criminal Law and Criminology* 83 (2): 338–363.
Crank, J. P., and R. Langworthy. 1996. "Fragmented Centralization and the Organization of the Police." *Policing and Society* 6 (3): 213–229.
Diamantopoulos, A., P. Riefler, and K. P. Roth. 2008. "Advancing Formative Measurement Models." *Journal of Business Research* 61 (12): 1203–1218.
DiMaggio, P. J., and W. W. Powell. 1983. "The Iron Cage Revisited: Institutional Isomorphism and Collective Rationality in Organizational Fields." *American Sociological Review* 48 (2): 147–160.
Donaldson, L. 1995. *American Anti-Management Theories of Organizations: A Critique of Paradigm Proliferation*. New York: Cambridge University Press.

Falcone, D. N., and L. E. Wells. 1995. "The County Sheriff as a Distinctive Policing Modality." *American Journal of Police* 14 (3/4): 123–149.

Giblin, M. J. 2006. "Structural Elaboration and Institutional Isomorphism: The Case of Crime Analysis Units." *Policing: An International Journal of Police Strategies & Management* 29 (4): 643–664.

Giblin, M. J., and G. W. Burruss. 2009. "Developing a Measurement Model of Institutional Processes in Policing." *Policing: An International Journal of Police Strategies & Management* 32 (2): 351–376.

Giblin, M. J., J. A. Schafer, and G. W. Burruss. 2009. "Homeland Security in the Heartland: Risk, Preparedness, and Organizational Capacity." *Criminal Justice Policy Review* 20 (3): 274–289.

Hassell, K. D., J. S. Zhao, and E. R. Maguire. 2003. "Structural Arrangements in Large Municipal Police Organizations: Revisiting Wilson's Theory of Local Political Culture." *Policing: An International Journal of Police Strategies and Management* 26 (2): 231–250.

Hu, L., and P. M. Bentler. 1999. "Cutoff Criteria for Fit Indexes in Covariance Structure Analysis: Conventional Criteria versus New Alternatives." *Structural Equation Modeling: A Multidisciplinary Journal* 6 (1): 1–55.

Hunt, R. G., and J. M. Magenau. 1993. *Power and the Police Chief: An Institutional and Organizational Analysis*. Newbury Park, CA: Sage.

Katz, C. M. 1997. "Police and Gangs: A Study of a Police Gang Unit." PhD diss., University of Nebraska Omaha.

Katz, C. M. 2001. "The Establishment of a Police Gang Unit: An Examination of Organizational Factors." *Criminology* 39 (1): 37–74.

Katz, C. M., E. R. Maguire, and D. W. Roncek. 2002. "The Creation of Specialized Police Gang Units." *Policing: An International Journal of Police Strategies and Management* 25 (3): 472–506.

King, W. R. 2014. "Organizational Failure and the Disbanding of Local Police Agencies." *Crime & Delinquency* 60 (5): 667–692.

Langworthy, R. H. 1985. "Wilson's Theory of Police Behavior: A Replication of the Constraint Theory." *Justice Quarterly* 2 (1): 89–98.

Lawrence, P. R., and J. W. Lorsch. 1967. *Organization and Environment: Managing Differentiation and Integration*. Cambridge, MA: Harvard University Press.

Liederbach, J., and L. F. Travis. 2008. "Wilson Redux: Another Look at Varieties of Police Behavior." *Police Quarterly* 11 (4): 447–467.

Maguire, E. R. 1997. "Structural Change in Large Municipal Police Organizations during the Community Policing Era." *Justice Quarterly* 14 (3): 701–730.

Maguire, E. R. 2014. "Police Organizations and the Iron Cage of Rationality." In *The Oxford Handbook of Police and Policing*, edited by M. D. Reisig and R. J. Kane, 68–98. New York: Oxford University Press.

Maguire, E. R., and C. M. Katz. 2002. "Community Policing, Loose Coupling, and Sensemaking in American Police Agencies." *Justice Quarterly* 19 (3): 503–536.

Maguire, E. R., and W. R. King. 2007. "The Changing Landscape of American Police Organizations." In *Policing 2020: Exploring the Future of Crime, Communities, and Policing*, edited by J. A. Schafer, 337–371. Washington, DC: Federal Bureau of Investigation.

Maguire, E. R., and S. D. Mastrofski. 2000. "Patterns of Community Policing in the United States." *Police Quarterly* 3 (1): 4–45.

Maguire, E. R., and C. D. Uchida. 2000. "Measurement and Explanation in the Comparative Study of American Police Organizations." In *Criminal Justice 2000: Vol 4. Measurement and Analysis of Crime and Justice*, edited by D. Duffee, D. McDowall, B. Ostrom, R. Crutchfield, S. Mastrofski, and L. Mazerolle, 491–557. Washington, DC: National Institute of Justice.

Maguire, E. R., C. D. Uchida, and K. Hassell. 2015. "Problem-Oriented Policing in Colorado Springs: A Content Analysis of 753 Cases." *Crime and Delinquency* 61 (1): 71–95.

Mastrofski, S. D. 1998. "Community Policing and Police Organization Structure." In *How to Recognize Good Policing: Problems and Issues*, edited by J. Brodeur, 161–189. Thousand Oaks, CA: Sage.

Mastrofski, S. D., R. R. Ritti, and D. Hoffmaster. 1987. "Organizational Determinants of Police Discretion: The Case of Drinking-Driving." *Journal of Criminal Justice* 15 (5): 387–402.

Matusiak, M. C. 2013. "The Dimensionality and Effect of Institutional Environment upon Police Leaders." PhD diss., Sam Houston State University.

Matusiak, M. C. 2014. "Dimensionality of Local Police Chiefs' Institutional Sovereigns." *Policing and Society: An International Journal of Research and Policy*. doi:10.1080/10439463.2014.989156.

Matusiak, M. C., B. A. Campbell, and W. R. King. 2014. "The Legacy of LEMAS: Effects on Police Scholarship of a Federally Administered, Multi-Wave Establishment Survey." *Policing: An International Journal of Police Strategies & Management* 37 (3): 630–648.

Meyer, J. W., and B. Rowan. 1977. "Institutionalized Organizations: Formal Structure as Myth and Ceremony." *American Journal of Sociology* 83 (2): 340–363.

Muthén, L. K., and B. O. Muthén. 1998–2012. *Mplus User's Guide*. 7th ed. Angeles, CA: Muthén & Muthén.

Reiss, A. J., Jr., and D. J. Bordua. 1967. "Environment and Organization: A Perspective on the Police." In *The Police: Six Sociological Essays*, edited by D. J. Bordua, 22–55. New York: Wiley.

Roberts, A., and J. M. Roberts, Jr. 2009. "Impact of Network Ties on Change in Police Agency Practices." *Policing: An International Journal of Police Strategies and Management* 32 (1): 38 55.

Schafer, J. A. 2013. *Effective Leadership in Policing: Successful Traits and Habits*. Durham, NC: Carolina Academic Press.

Schulz, D. M. 2003. "Women Police Chiefs: A Statistical Profile." *Police Quarterly* 6 (3): 330–345.

Scott, W. R. 1987. "The Adolescence of Institutional Theory." *Administrative Science Quarterly* 32 (4): 493–511.

Scott, W. R. 2008. "Lords of the Dance: Professionals as Institutional Agents." *Organization Studies* 29 (2): 219–238.

Slovak, J. 1986. *Styles of Urban Policing: Organization, Environment, and Police Styles in Selected American Cities*. New York: New York University Press.

Smith, B. W., and M. D. Holmes. 2003. "Community Accountability, Minority Threat, and Police Brutality: An Examination of Civil Rights Criminal Complaints." *Criminology* 41 (4): 1035–1064.

Stucky, T. D. 2005. "Local Politics and Police Strength." *Justice Quarterly* 22 (2): 139–169.

Suchman, M. C. 1995. "Managing Legitimacy: Strategic and Institutional Approaches." *The Academy of Management Review* 20 (3): 571–610.

Thompson, J. D. 1967. *Organizations in Action*. New York: McGraw-Hill.

Thompson, J. D., and W. J. McEwen. 1958. "Organizational Goals and Environment: Goal Setting as an Interaction Process." *American Sociological Review* 23 (1): 23–31.

Vitale, A. S. 2005. "Innovation and Institutionalization: Factors in the Development of 'Quality of Life' Policing in New York City." *Policing and Society* 15 (2): 99–124.

Willis, J. J. 2011. "Enhancing Police Legitimacy by Integrating Compstat and Community Policing." *Policing: An International Journal of Police Strategies and Management* 34 (4): 654–673.

Willis, J. J., and S. D. Mastrofski. 2011. "Innovations in Policing: Meanings, Structures, and Processes." *Annual Review of Law and Social Science* 7: 309–334.

Willis, J. J., S. D. Mastrofski, and D. Weisburd. 2007. "Making Sense of COMPSTAT: A Theory-Based Analysis of Organizational Change in Three Police Departments." *Law and Society Review* 41 (1): 147–188.

Wilson, J. Q. 1968. *Varieties of Police Behavior: The Management of Law and Order in Eight Communities*. Cambridge, MA: Harvard University Press.

Worrall, J. L. 2010. "Is Blue Going Green?" *Journal of Criminal Justice* 38 (4): 506–511.

Yu, C. 2002. "Evaluating Cutoff Criteria of Model Fit Indices for Latent Variable Models with Binary and Continuous Outcomes." PhD diss., University of California Los Angeles.

Zhao, J. S. 1994. "Contemporary Organizational Change in Community-Oriented Policing: A Contingency Approach." PhD diss., Washington State University.

Zhao, J., N. He, and N. Lovrich. 2006. "The Effect of Local Political Culture on Policing Behaviors in the 1990s: A Retest of Wilson's Theory in More Contemporary Times." *Journal of Criminal Justice* 34 (6): 569–578.

Zhao, J., N. P. Lovrich, and T. H. Robinson. 2001. "Community Policing: Is It Changing the Basic Functions of Policing?" *Journal of Criminal Justice* 29 (5): 365–377.

Zhao, J., L. Ren, and N. Lovrich. 2010. "Wilson's Theory of Local Political Culture Revisited in Today's Police Organizations." *Policing: An International Journal of Police Strategies and Management* 33 (2): 287–304.

Appendix 1. Items used to construct composite measures of seven environmental sectors

Federal/state law enforcement
State law enforcement agency
Federal law enforcement agency
Federal Department of Justice
Department of Homeland Security
State Attorney General
Texas Department of Criminal Justice

National media
New York Times
Washington Post
Wall Street Journal
National TV or Radio News

Local media
Small or local newspaper
Local TV news

Police employee associations

Officers' union
Combined Law Enforcement Associations of Texas
Texas Municipal Police Association
Fraternal Order of Police

Elected officials

Local, elected representative
State, elected representative
Federal, elected representative

Local criminal justice organizations

Local law enforcement agencies
Local county sheriff
Municipal/Justice of the Peace Court
County prosecutor
Local/Regional crime lab

Local emergency medical organizations

EMS or Fire services
Local hospitals

Active representation and police response to sexual assault complaints

Melissa Schaefer Morabito, April Pattavina and Linda M. Williams

ABSTRACT

Policing has long been a profession dominated by white males. Yet, the organizational literature suggests that diverse public sector organizations are essential to a well-functioning democracy. Representative bureaucracy theory is the idea that public agencies should mirror the society in which it functions in order to best meet the needs of its citizens. There are three necessary conditions in order for representative bureaucracy theory to be applicable to a problem. First, bureaucrats must have discretion in decision-making. Next, bureaucrats must exercise discretion in a policy area that has important implications for the group they represent. Finally, bureaucrats must be directly associated with the decisions they make. Given that police work requires extraordinary discretion, representation holds great importance for police organizations. There has, however, been scant literature examining the interaction between representation, organizational characteristics of police agencies, and situational characteristics of sexual assault incidents. This paper builds upon previous research regarding the effect of diversity on public safety outcomes. A national sample of police organizations reporting to both LEMAS and NIBRS will be used with specific attention paid to interaction between organizational characteristics, agency innovativeness, and representation.

Despite serving diverse communities, policing has long been a profession dominated by white males. In 1987, women comprised 7.5% of the sworn police employees and by 2000 this had increased to 10.6%. Unfortunately, the gains in the percentage of female police officers have not kept up at the previous pace and, in fact, have slowed between 2000 and 2007, moving from 10.6 to 11.9% (Reaves 2010). Over time, police departments have remained largely gendered organizations (Shelley, Morabito, and Tobin-Gurley 2011) dominated by white males. Yet, the organizational literature suggests that diverse public sector organizations are essential to both effective agencies as well as a well-functioning democracy (Smith and Monaghan 2013). This lack of gender diversity in policing may also affect organizational outputs – namely police responses to crimes against women – sexual assaults.

Representative bureaucracy theory is based on the premise that public agencies should mirror the communities they serve in order to best meet the needs of its citizens (Mosher 1982; Van Riper 1958, 552). Passive representation is indicated by the actual composition of employees working in the organization as compared to the community served. Active representation refers to how this composition affects policy outputs – the inclusion of a diverse group of employees affects the way the organization conducts business. The opportunity for active representation is hindered when there is no passive representation; for example, when women are only included in the organization in only a token capacity. There has, however, been limited empirical research applying representative bureaucracy theory to policing. In particular, there exists scant literature that examines the interaction between the organizational characteristics of police agencies, representation of women in the community, situational characteristics of criminal offenses with the arrests, and clearances of crimes against this population (for exceptions see Theobald and Haider-Markel [2009]; Schuck and Rabe-Hemp [2014]).

To expand our knowledge of the role of representation in the outcomes of police organizations, this paper builds upon previous research regarding the effect of organizational characteristics including diversity in combination with situational characteristics on public safety outcomes such as arrests and clearance rates. According to representative bureaucracy theory, agencies that passively represent the communities that they serve should have also achieved some measure of active representation. This means that even when controlling for incident-level measures, female representation in a police agency affects arrest and clearance rates. Specifically, we will look at outcomes in crimes against women – namely sexual assaults to test the utility of representative bureaucracy theory in a police setting. We examine what factors affect the likelihood of arrest and clearance of sexual assault crimes including the passive representation of women in police organizations in a sworn capacity. A national sample of police organizations reporting to both the Law Enforcement Management and Administrative Statistics survey (LEMAS) and the National Incident Based Reporting System (NIBRS) will be used with specific attention paid to organizational characteristics, agency innovativeness, and representation.

Review of the literature and theoretical foundation

Representative bureaucracy

The absence of women in police organizations is a well-documented problem as the progress of women in police organizations has stalled (Cordner and Cordner 2011). The recruitment and selection of women has seemingly not been a priority for police departments with most lacking any efforts attract female candidates. Specifically, Jordan et al. (2009) found in their national survey on police agency employment and recruitment practices, 'only one in five agencies have targeted recruitment strategies for women and minorities' (333). In short, police departments do not represent the gender diversity of the communities that they serve.

There are two types of representation discussed in this literature: passive and active representation. Passive representation is indicated by the actual composition of employees working in the organization and how it matches the community served. Much of the research examining passive representation is descriptive in nature detailing the racial and socioeconomic status of bureaucratic employees (Kennedy 2012). More recently, Morabito and Shelley (2015) examined the correlates of diversity of women and racial minorities using a framework informed by representative bureaucracy theory. While this research sheds light on the differences in gender and minority representation across police agencies (Morabito and Shelley 2015), it does not offer evidence of any variation in outcomes across these agencies. In short, there is scant research that examines whether passive representation in criminal justice agencies translates into active representation.

Active representation refers to how this composition affects policy outputs – whether the inclusion of a diverse group of employees affects the way the organization conducts business. In fact, a central theme of representative bureaucracy is the assumption that passive representation will lead to active representation, whereby bureaucrats act purposely on behalf of their counterparts in the general population (Pitkin 1967). To understand how the passive representation of women might have active consequences, we turn to the criminological and criminal justice literatures. For example, Schuck and Rabe-Hemp (2014) propose the disruption thesis to explain how increasing gender diversity in policing may affect organizational outcomes for police agencies. The disruption thesis posts that by increasing the number of women in police organizations, cultural values shift and the organization becomes less insular. This cultural change results in conflict such as interpersonal disputes and incivilities. Conflict results in mistrust, hostility, and resentment that affects group cohesion creating an opportunity for change that is ultimately capitalized upon by management. Thus, the 'disruption' is caused by hiring more women which forces police agencies to change their policies, procedures, and structures. Farrell (2015) extends the disruption hypothesis further arguing that as women move into positions of authority, norms are challenged. The inclusion of more women as police officers would reduce the differential treatment of women as offenders – but this could also apply to reception of female victims. Meier and Nicholson-Crotty (2006) posit several theories of why female representation might increase the number of reported assaults to police. They make the argument that the active representation of female officers results in bringing awareness to male officers about crimes against women such as sexual assault. Alternatively, female victims might feel more comfortable sharing details of a sexual assault with a female officer which could result in a more complete investigation. Regardless of the explanation, these theories all rely on the premise that the passive representation of women in police organizations results in active representation. What is missing from these theories, however, is the number or proportion of women needed in a police agency to reap the desired changes. It is unclear if the general increase in passive representation results in a corresponding increase in active representation or if there is a 'tipping point' of representation that when reached outcomes subsequently change.

Active representation is not only driven by the individual officers making decisions that are better for women but also by the structure of the organization. This is because officers' use of discretion is affected not only by individual characteristics but also by agency structures and processes (Farrell 2015). These structures and processes give officers more or less discretion and affect how outcomes are attributed to individual officers (Meier and Bohte 2001). Much of the public administration literature focuses on active representation in educational institutions (c.f. Meier and Bohte 2001; Sowa and Selden 2003) and among those researchers there is disagreement on how to measure organizational discretion. It also may be that given missions and responsibilities that are unique to educational institutions, that the structures and processes that are linked to discretion may be somewhat different than in policing. For example, the unique collective bargaining structure of policing may affect processes thereby influencing discretion (Morabito 2014). Police officers are represented by a wide variety of union and bargaining agreements differ substantially within and across agencies (Doerner and Doerner 2010). Research on the adoption of new programs and policies suggests that size and budget are crucial because they give police agencies slack resources (Morabito 2010). We might expect that agencies with these slack resources can devote them to diverse recruitment and training.

In policing, discretion can be affected by the traditional nature of the agency. In her exploration of police response to hate crimes, Farrell (2014) notes that not all police departments are equally successful at making changes in response to community demands or a changing legal landscape. Some police organizations are 'pervious' or susceptible to the process of organizational change in response to these types of changes (Jenness and Grattet 2005). Previous literature has examined the creation of hate crime units or designated personnel as measures of perviousness because these changes are responsive to legislation criminalizing the offenses and community demand (Farrell 2014; Jenness and Grattet 2005). If a department is responsive to hate crime, they might also be responsive to changes in attitude regarding crimes against women. Thus, legislative changes such as mandatory arrest laws might have an impact as well. It might be expected that active representation could flourish in organizations that are more pervious – or susceptible to the disruption that diverse employees are hypothesized to cause. More traditional police agencies tend to have a great deal of vertical differentiation – many layers of management as well as functional differentiation – a large number of special units (Morabito 2010). Both functional and vertical differentiations result in carefully delineated responsibilities both across the agency and down the hierarchy. These delineated job tasks translate into reduced discretion for police officers.

Yet, it is clear that passive representation does not always result in active representation (Pitts 2005). There are two major studies that have specifically examined the effects of active representation in policing. First, a study conducted by Wilkins and Williams (2008) on the impact of hiring African-American officers on racial profiling did not support the proposition that passive representation leads to outcomes associated with active representation. The researchers found that an increase in African-American officers (i.e., passive representation) was correlated with a simultaneous increase in racial disparities in traffic stops. Conversely, Meier and Nicholson-Crotty (2006) find that police agencies that employ larger numbers of female officers file more sexual assault reports and make more sexual assault arrests. While this research suggests that passive representation of women in police agencies has positive active consequences for crimes that impact women, there are a number of concerns about this study that make these findings surprising. First, Meier and Nicholson-Crotty focused only on urban areas – not typical of policing in the United States particularly as it relates to policing sexual assault. Barriers to accessing services including the police differ for rural and urban victims (cf. Logan et al. 2005). The importance of incident, perpetrator, and victim characteristics varies across geographic areas in the victim decision to report (Rennison, Dragiewicz, and DeKeseredy 2013) as well as public expectations of the police (Jiao 2001). As such, an investigation of the factors that affect sexual assault outcomes should include incidents from rural, urban, and suburban jurisdictions. Next, they did not compare arrest to other outcomes – only across departments. Of greater concern is that while Meier and Nicholson-Crotty included measures of community context, they failed to include incident-level characteristics or indicators of the police organization. Research suggests that incident-level characteristics are highly correlated with sexual assault outcomes – perhaps explaining most of the variation in criminal justice outcomes (cf. Pattavina, Morabito, and Williams 2016; Spohn and Tellis 2012). In addition, police agencies have different organizational structures and histories with the adoption of innovative practices that may affect police practices independently of the diversity of their personnel.

Police response to sexual assault

The police response to victims of sexual assault has been well documented in the media (Reilly 2015) and by researchers (Spohn and Tellis 2012). While most sexual assaults are never reported to the police, for victims that do report, their cases rarely result in arrest. In fact, evidence suggests that there exists substantial attrition in sexual assault cases reported to the police (Spohn and Tellis 2012). The recent work by Spohn and Tellis (2012) conducted in Los Angeles considered how official reporting standards for classifying the way cases are cleared or solved by police (using Uniform Crime Reporting [UCR] standards) were applied to incidents of sexual assault. According to their report, 46% of sexual assault incidents reported to the Los Angeles police department were officially classified as cleared or solved by the police. Though 'solved,' many of these incidents (33.5% of all cases or 73% of the cleared cases) did not actually result in an arrest, but instead were cleared 'by exceptional means' and no arrest was made. Research conducted with police agencies across the US documents that between 12 and 45% of cases reported to the police will result in an arrest (Alderden and Ullman 2012; Bouffard 2000; Spohn and Tellis 2012).

As evidenced by these numbers, individual police officers have a great deal of discretion in how sexual assault complaints are pursued. Existing research on police discretion suggests that the police decision to arrest for sexual assault offenses can be influenced by a variety of legal and extralegal factors that are largely related to the incident (Tasca et al. 2012). These legal and extralegal factors can affect the outcomes of sexual assault cases (Alderden and Ullman 2012; Kerstetter 1990; Spohn and Tellis 2012). Legal factors are those that indicate evidence of a crime (i.e., witnesses, weapons used, or physical evidence) as defined by statute. Evidence suggests that the weapons and injuries are highly correlated with the police decision to arrest (cf. Kerstetter 1990; Spohn and Tellis 2012). Similarly, when sexual assault occurs in concert with another crime, police are more likely to make an arrest (Kerstetter 1990; Lafree 1989). Extra-legal factors are legally irrelevant victim, suspect, or other characteristics associated with an incident. In particular, research suggests that extralegal factors – such as the relationship between the victim and the offender can influence the outcome of sexual assault cases with police more likely to pursue cases where the victim and suspect are strangers (cf. Du Mont, Miller, and Myhr 2003; Lafree 1989). The use of drugs by a victim has been shown to reduce the likelihood of cases moving forward in the criminal justice system (Beichner and Spohn 2012). Victim race has also been identified as an important predictor of sexual assault case outcomes but is inconsistent across studies (Lafree 1989; Tellis and Spohn 2008) as has whether the assault occurs in private residence or in public (Spohn and Tellis 2012).

Individual officers alone, however, are not entirely responsible for the outcomes in cases involving crimes against women. Studies comparing the behavior of male and female officers have typically focused on differences in the decision-making of individual officers without regard to the organizational contexts in which these gendered decisions occur (Farrell 2015). King (2000) suggests that organizational context can be crucial for understanding differences in the implementation of new police innovations. Police department structures are important for understanding the representativeness of organizations (Jordan et al. 2009; Zhao, He, and Lovrich 2005) as well as agency outcomes. For example, the size of the organization is an important explanatory variable. Some research suggests that smaller police departments are less likely to have turnover among employees and therefore may be less representative of the community (Zhao, He, and Lovrich 2005). This lack of turnover means that female officers might be more difficult to hire – fewer slots result in less diversity. Morabito (2008) suggests that budget may also be a proxy for the 'slack resources' which might be related to an enhanced relationship to the clearance of crimes against women like sexual assault.

In addition to size and budget, one should consider the level of vertical differentiation present in the agency. Vertical differentiation refers to the layers of bureaucracy within the agency and gives an approximation of the height of the organization providing information about the formal structure of the agency (Maguire 2003). The more the vertical differentiation, the less likely the agency is adaptable to change. Difficulty in adapting to change as represented by vertical differentiation may be indicative of an overall resistance to diversification or allocating responses to the investigation of sexual assaults. Similarly, the more structured the organization, the more barriers that may exist to altering practices. Functional differentiation refers to the degree to which tasks are broken down to into functionally distinct units. Occupational differentiation is indicative of the extent to which specially trained workers are used to meet the organizational goals (Langworthy 1986; Maguire 1997). Agencies that have many special units are more functionally differentiated than those that do not. The relationship between functional differentiation and closure of sex crimes complaints is unclear.

The adoption of previous new programs may also influence the response of police departments to crimes against women. Jenness and Grattet (2005) suggest that some police organizations are 'pervious' or susceptible to the process of organizational change in response to the passage of new law. They suggest two main factors that predict susceptibility to change – police organization exposure to the influence of community demands, and the alignment of legal change with existing practices and policies of the organization (Farrell 2014). Another important factor that contributes to the organizational landscape is collective bargaining. Collective bargaining has been included in previous studies of the adoption of innovation because it is indicative of the organizational environment (Morabito 2014; Wilson 2005). Previous investigations have found that collective bargaining also affects the ability of municipal employees to wield influence over local politicians regarding wages, job security, and general employment issues (Mehay and Gonzalez 1994).

The nexus between representative bureaucracy theory and police response to sexual assault

Rich and Seffrin (2014) note that rape is a highly gendered crime as the majority of victims are women. This represents somewhat of a mismatch – male police officers and female victims. It has been hypothesized that increasing female police representation may lead to more arrests for crimes against women because female officers will be more empathetic toward female victims and may take these crimes more seriously (Stalans and Finn 2000). As a result, female officers are often assigned to rape cases, making sexual assault investigation correspondingly gendered (Archbold and Schulz 2008; Garcia 2003; Rabe-Hemp 2009). There is mixed evidence as to the attitudes of female officers about rape cases (Alderden and Ullman 2012, Rich and Seffrin 2014).

In a recent examination of police response to sexual assault, Walfield (2016) uses multilevel logistic regression to explore how incident, victim, offender, and police department characteristics influence the type of clearance using data from two national data-sets: NIBRS and the LEMAS. Similar to previous research (Meier and Nicholson-Crotty 2006), Walfield (2016) finds that an increase in the percentage of female officers increases the odds of arrest. While, this was an elegantly designed study, several important constructs were not included in the model. Specifically, collective bargaining, legislative environment, agency structure (functional and vertical differentiations), perviousness, and agency size were excluded from the sample. Furthermore, it is unclear if agencies were included in the sample that may not be primary responders to calls for service.

Thus, while Walfield (2016) and Meier and Nicholson-Crotty (2006) have explored the effect of female officers on case outcomes, neither has used fully specified models. As such, police response to sexual assault represents an interesting test for representative bureaucracy theory. Meier and Stewart (1992) propose that there are three necessary conditions in order for representative bureaucracy to be applicable to a problem. First, bureaucrats must have discretion in the decision-making. Next, these bureaucrats must exercise this discretion in a policy area that has important implications for the group they represent. Finally, these bureaucrats must be directly associated with the decisions they make. These conditions clearly apply to the police in their response to sexual assaults. In particular, police officers have a great deal of discretion as part of their response to sexual assault cases (Bouffard 2000) – a crime that overwhelmingly affects women. The decision to arrest and/or clear crimes perpetrated against women has enormous consequences for the community and for holding offenders accountable for criminal activity. This discretion begins with the preliminary investigation conducted by the original patrol officer who arrives on scene to respond to the complainant and often ends with the secondary investigation conducted by a detective. While, police managers do not hold individual responding patrol officers accountable for whether an arrest is eventually made, ultimately their success or failure in response to these cases is reflected in clearance rates for the agency.

Once a case is reported to the police and investigated, it can be open and inactive if investigation is continuing or it can be cleared. Cases that are open and inactive may lack the evidence necessary to identify a suspect. Police can choose to leave the case open in hopes that new evidence will emerge after the initial report. The other outcome is clearance and there are two clearance categories that can be used by the police. These categories are *cleared by arrest* and *cleared by exceptional means*. According to the UCR Handbook (2004, 80), a case may be exceptionally cleared if the following criteria are met: (a) the police have definitely established the identity of the offender; (b) there is enough information to support an arrest, charge, and turning over to the court for prosecution; (c) the exact location of the offender is known so that the subject can be taken into custody; and (d) There is some reason outside law enforcement control that precludes arresting, charging, and prosecuting the offender.

The use of the exceptional clearance category to close a case was originally intended for those rare cases where an offender is known and probable cause exists for arrest, but due to circumstances beyond the control of law enforcement, no arrest is made (Feeney 2000). Exceptional clearance is used however in other circumstances such as when a victim refuses to cooperate or the prosecutor declines the case. According to Spohn and Tellis (2012), 45.7% of sexual assault incidents reported to the police in Los Angeles, CA were officially classified as cleared or solved by the police. Many of these incidents (33.5% of all cases), however, did not result in an arrest, but instead were cleared using a UCR exceptional means classification. In analyzing a sample of 842 agencies reporting to the NIBRS and 15,279 incidents of sexual assault, sodomy, and sexual assault with an object, Pattavina, Morabito, and Williams (2016) found that the percentage of female officers in police agencies was unrelated to the use of exceptional clearance. The lack of relationship exists for both cases where victims refuse to cooperate and the prosecutor declines the case. While a suspect is known to the police in cases cleared by exceptional means, no arrest was ever made and the case was closed (Pattavina, Morabito, and Williams 2016). Thus for victims, there is no difference between clearance by exceptional means, inactive or even open since none of these statuses result in arrest.

In making these decisions, police agencies must also work within the constraints of the legislative environment which is also an important consideration in understanding the police response to crimes against women. As Winfree and DeJong (2015) note, 'sworn officers, like any downstream bureaucratic stakeholders, take their behavioral cues for action from those upstream. If the police perceive (or misperceive) that new laws and policies give them license to act against or ignore the interests of women' …, they might do so. In short, legislation that mandates arrest in domestic violence cases can increase both reports of and the likelihood of an arrest (Simpson et al. 2006).

The police response to sexual assault offers the opportunity to test whether passive representation translates into active representation of women who are victims of sexual assault.

Hypotheses

Taking into account the organizational environment as well as the situational elements of criminal activity, the following hypotheses will be explored:

(1) The passive representation of women in police organizations in a sworn capacity translates into greater active representation of female citizens in the community. Active representation is measured as
   (a) Greater arrest in sexual assault complaints and
   (b) Overall clearance of crimes against women, namely sexual assaults in the community
(2) Organizational factors affect the clearance of sexual assault cases
(3) Variation in sexual assault outcomes can largely be explained by incident-level factors.

Data and methods

The present study draws a national sample of 152 police jurisdictions of varying size and composition in a cross-sectional investigation using data merged from the agency-level 2007 LEMAS surveys, and combined incident-level details from 2007 and 2008 NIBRS extract files. Analyses include all municipal police departments that are first responders to 911 calls and therefore regularly interact with the community in the United States regardless of their size but who also report to NIBRS and LEMAS. Departments that do not have primary law enforcement responsibilities were removed from the sample. From NIBRS, 18,730 incidents of sexual assault incidents were included. This includes sexual assault, sexual assault with object, sodomy, and forcible fondling incidents with female victims over the age of 13 and where the offender was not a family member.

The two dependent variables are the outcome for the sexual assault cases: case open or exceptionally cleared as compared to arrest. Hierarchical logistic regression was conducted to determine the odds that the representation of women affects the likelihood that a sexual assault case remains open or ends in exceptional clearance relative to arrest.

Independent variables

Organizational indicators

The key measure in this investigation is the proportion of full-time female officers in the police department. We also examined whether there was a tipping point – meaning that a department must have a certain proportion of women in the department for changes to occur. We created a variable with a tipping point of 12% as this is the national average for the proportion of women in policing (Reaves 2010).

The next organizational measure is that of vertical differentiation focuses on the height of the organization (Langworthy 1986; Maguire 1997). It has been defined as the social space between the top and the bottom levels of the organization (Maguire 2003). Specifically, as suggested by Maguire et al. (1997), vertical differentiation is measured as follows: Vertical Differentiation (Height) (Salary of Chief – Salary of Entry Officer)/Salary of Entry Officer. Functional differentiation refers to the degree to which tasks are broken down to into functionally distinct units and occupational differentiation is indicative of the extent to which specially trained workers are used (Langworthy 1986; Maguire 1997). Functional differentiation is measured as an additive index of the special units in the police department.

Perviousness is measured by a dichotomous variable noting whether the police department has a bias unit or dedicated personnel (1 = yes, 0 = no). Collective bargaining has similarly been measured dichotomously where 1 = sworn officers with collective bargaining rights and 0 = no collective bargaining rights. The number of sworn officers and size of the budget are important factors in determining how and in what manner police resources will be deployed (Zhao, He, and Lovrich 2005). The variable officers represent the number of full-time sworn officers, an agency employed during the current fiscal year per 1000 citizens. This is a continuous variable. Budget represents the agency budget for the current fiscal year in proportion to the population size (this translates to dollar per person in the population).

We have also included a measure of legislative context. Some states have laws that mandate officers make an arrest in domestic violence situations. Other states have preferred arrest policies, where officers are directed to err on the side of a more formal response. Finally, there are states that direct officers to use their own discretion in domestic violence cases. This variable is constructed as a binary variable where mandatory arrest equals 1 and all other statutes are 0. These data were collected from the American Bar Association Commission on Domestic Violence.

Incident characteristics

Indicators of crime are also included as indicators of the likelihood of arrest. Legal factors included in the model are if there were injuries noted in the police report, whether or not there was a weapon (including a gun, knife, or other weapons) used, and if there was another crime that co-occurred. These are coded as binary variables (yes/no). Extralegal factors were also included in the analysis. Specifically, we measure the relationship between the victim and the offender in two categories: acquaintance or intimate partner. These were coded as binary individual variables (yes/no). We also include whether the assault occurred in a residential location as binary variables (yes/no) and whether the victim was under the influence of drugs (yes/no). Finally, victim age (continuous) and race (white/non-white) were included in the model.

Findings

Descriptive statistics are included in Table 1.[1] As displayed in Table 1, of the 152 agencies, 50% are located in states with mandatory arrest laws. In 54% of agencies, officers have collective bargaining rights. Ninety-five percent of agencies display characteristics of perviousness. The mean for vertical differentiation is 1.4 with a standard deviation of 0.57. The proportion of female officers in the agency had a mean of 0.11 with a standard deviation of 0.04, which is in line with the national average for female representation in police agencies. Thirty-two percent of departments in the sample were above the designated tipping point – meaning that 12% or more of officers were female. For the departments in our sample, the mean ratio of officers to community is 2.15 officers per 1000 citizens with a standard deviation of 0.79.

For these 152 agencies, 18,730 incidents of sexual assault met the criteria to be included in the analyses. Of these incidents, 81% involved the use of a weapon and 26% involved an injury. Seventeen percent of incidents involved an intimate partner as the perpetrator while 64% involved an acquaintance and 19% a stranger. Nine percent of sexual assaults occurred in concert with another crime. Sixty percent occurred in a personal residence and 32% of victims were non-white. Twelve percent of cases involved the use of drugs. The average age of a victim of sexual assault is 25 with a standard deviation of 12. For the dependent variable, only 18% of cases ended in arrest. Sixty-eight percent of cases remained open and 14% were exceptionally cleared.

Table 1. Descriptive statistics.

	Percent (%)	Mean	Std. Dev	Min	Max
Agency characteristics (N = 152)					
Mandatory arrest law	50	0.5	0.5	0	1
Collective bargaining	54	0.54	0.5	0	1
Perviousness	95	0.95	0.22	0	1
Vertical differentiation		1.4	0.57	0.24	4.75
Functional differentiation		15.39	4.36	1	22
Proportion of female officers		0.11	0.04	0.03	0.27
Officers		2.15	0.79	0.86	6.61
Tipping point		0.32	0.47	0	1
Incident characteristics (N = 18,730)					
Weapon	81			0	1
Intimate partner	17			0	1
Acquaintance	64			0	1
Stranger	20			0	1
Crime co-occurrence	9			0	1
Residence location	60			0	1
Victim race	32			0	1
Injury	26			0	1
Arrest	18				
Open	68				
Exceptionally cleared	12				
Age (mean, std. dev.)		25	12	13	90
Drugs	12			0	1

Hierarchical logistic regression was used to determine the likelihood that female representation among the rank and file increases the likelihood that sexual assault complaints end in arrest as compared to keeping the case open or exceptional clearance as well as the effects of situational factors. These results are displayed in Table 2.

As displayed in Table 2, there are both organizational and situational indicators that predict the way police agencies handle sexual assault crimes suggesting support for the second and third hypotheses. In this table, arrest in a sexual assault complaint is the reference category. First, only one of the organizational characteristics is somewhat in line with expectations based on the literature. Agencies that exhibit perviousness or are more innovative are less likely (−0.431) to keep sexual assault complaints open as compared to making an arrest. The data suggest that perviousness is unrelated to the exceptional clearance.

Some surprising findings include unionization Collective bargaining in police agencies is associated with a reduced likelihood (−0.738) of keeping cases open as compared to arrest. It is less surprising that collective bargaining is also associated with an increased likelihood (2.544) of exceptionally clearing sexual assault complaints – as compared to arrest when other factors are controlled. Vertical differentiation or the height of the organization decreases both the likelihood of cases remaining open as compared to arrest (−0.828) and exceptional clearance (−0.584). Functional differentiation is unrelated to open cases but is negatively correlated (−0.902) meaning a decreased likelihood of incidents being exceptionally cleared as compared with arrest. Mandatory arrest laws and the number of sworn officers are unrelated to the likelihood that sexual assault complaints remain open or are exceptionally cleared as compared to arrest. Most notably, however, there is no support for our first hypotheses based on these data. The passive representation of women in police organizations in a sworn capacity does not appear to translate into greater active representation of female citizens in the community. Findings suggest that female officers do not decrease the odds that sexual assault complaints end in exceptional clearance or remain open as compared to arrest. There is also no evidence that when there is a tipping point – a critical mass of female officers – that there is any change. The tipping point of female officers was statistically unrelated to the likelihood of keeping the case open or exceptionally clearing it.

Not surprisingly, incident-level characteristics are more related to the decision to exceptionally clear or keep cases open. Victim relationship, acquaintance (1.663), and intimate partner (2.988) are both

Table 2. Hierarchical logistic regression predicting sexual assault case outcomes.

	Open	Exceptional clearance
	Odds ratio	Odds ratio
Agency characteristics (n = 152)		
Intercept	0.184**	6.305**
Functional differentiation	0.986	0.902**
Collective bargaining	0.738*	2.544**
Female officer representation	0.176	3.052
Perviousness	0.431*	0.541
Officers	1.111	1.408
Vertical differentiation	0.828*	0.584*
Mandatory arrest laws	1.295	0.593
Incident characteristics		
Weapon	1.148	1.061
Intimate partner	2.988**	0.666**
Acquaintance	1.663**	0.681**
Crime co-occurrence	2.060**	3.247**
Residence location	0.853**	0.746**
Victim race	0.973	1.148*
Injury	1.221**	1.668**
Victim age	0.999	0.991**
Drugs	1.218*	1.041
Year 2008	0.933	1.105
Pseudo R^2	0.07	0.15
Likelihood ratio	X^2 435, df 17**	X^2 321, df 17**

$^*p < 0.05$; $^{**}p < 0.01$.

correlated with an increased likelihood of keeping cases open as compared to arrest. Unexpectedly, cases involving both intimate partners (−0.666) and acquaintances (−0.581) are less likely to end in exceptional clearance than arrest. As expected, crime co-occurrence increases the likelihood of both keeping the case open (2.060) and exceptionally clearing the case (3.247) as compared to arrest. Residence location is also related to police outcomes. When the assault occurs in a residence as opposed to in public, the police are less likely to keep cases open or exceptionally clear them as compared to arrest.

Victim race was unrelated to the likelihood that cases were kept open but positively associated with exceptional clearance. A victim of color is more likely to have a case be cleared exceptionally than end in arrest. Injury was positively associated with the likelihood of keeping a case open (1.221) as well as the police use of exceptional clearance (1.668). Drugs were positively related with keeping cases open as compared to arrest (1.218) and unrelated to exceptional clearance. The presence of a weapon was unrelated to keeping the case open and exceptionally clearing the complaint. Surprisingly, victim age was unrelated to the likelihood of police deciding to keep a case open but was negatively related to exceptional clearance (−0.991). Police were less to exceptionally clear a case as victims increase in age.

Discussion

Despite recent research by Oberfield (2014), suggesting that representative bureaucracy theory holds great promise for explaining gendered differences in police behavior, this manuscript does not support its usefulness. He notes that 'officers from different backgrounds, despite undergoing roughly similar organizational experiences can emerge as different workers' (171). In short, the personal experiences that new recruits bring into the academy affect the ways that they do their jobs – well into their careers. These gendered differences may well in fact affect how police officers use their discretion. Despite the strong promise of representative bureaucracy theory, we find that in fact female representation does not enhance the criminal justice outcomes for victims of sexual assault. This finding is contrary to that of the previous research (cf. Meier and Nicholson-Crotty 2006; Walfield 2016). Previous research, however, relied on models that were not fully specified and ignored some of the crucial agency characteristics that explain how policies and new programs are implemented (cf. Morabito 2010).

There are a variety of other explanations for these finding. First, we can't ignore the stalled progress of women in policing in our discussion of representative bureaucracy. Female and minority police officers continue to meet with hostility in the work place (Haarr and Morash 1999; Morash and Haarr 1995; Walker 1985). Women are still relatively new to the policing profession and comprise a small minority of police officers. According to the LEMAS survey, in 2007, women made up only 11.96% of police officers nationally. The inability of police agencies to fully achieve a representative bureaucracy can be traced back to a long history of employment discrimination against women and minorities (Heidensohn 1992; Leinen 1984; Martin 1994). Some discrimination was reduced by Title VII of the 1964 Civil Rights Act and then by the 1972 Equal Employment Opportunity Act prohibiting employment discrimination on the basis of race, color, national origin, sex, and religion. In recent years, however, the progress of women and minority groups has stalled (Cordner and Cordner 2011; Reaves 2010) as many of the trailblazers retire from policing.

Alexander (2012) notes that newcomers entering into the existing hierarchy are required to exercise power in the same way and play by the same old rules and structures in order to succeed. This means that in more traditional agencies, female officers may have more difficulty exercising power. We considered that for disruption to occur as discussed by Schuck and Rabe-Hemp (2014) in response to sexual assault cases, the agency must have a specific proportion of female officers. It might be that in fact there is a tipping point. Evidence suggests that female police officers experience greater job satisfaction when the percentage of female officers increases (Krimmel and Gormley 2003). It may be that looking at female representation alone is not enough – instead female officers may need to reach a critical mass before they feel empowered to challenge traditional rules and policies and 'disrupt' the status quo. Our results, however, do not lend support for a tipping point. There are some limitations to this finding. We relied on 12% female as our tipping point as this is the national average, but perhaps this is just not high enough. There were not enough agencies that had substantially more female officers to reasonably conduct an analysis with a higher tipping point. Future research should further investigate the possibility of a higher tipping point.

The inhospitable environment for female officers likely translates to their treatment of women in the community. As women struggle for inclusion in policing, they may not have the power to control organizational treatment of women in the community. There exists the organizational presumption that victims of sexual assault are still viewed with skepticism by the police. Winfree and DeJong (2015) write

> attempts to delegitimize rape through the identification of real or legitimate victims, the use of extralegal factors to decide whether to make arrests or prosecute rape cases, and the failure of numerous colleges and universities to handle sexual assault cases appropriately are all important factors that limit women's freedom and keep victims from reporting their assaults to officials. (63)

Organizational factors had a limited but significant effect on the sexual assault outcomes. Notably, vertical and functional differentiation, each reduces the likelihood that a case will both remain open or be exceptionally cleared as compared to arrest. The mechanism by which this occurs is deserving of further attention in the literature. It is not surprising that the findings indicate that situational characteristics greatly predict the likelihood a case is cleared exceptionally or remains open. Similar to previous research, the relationship between the victim and the offender and the location where the crime occurs influences case outcomes. This means that non-legal incident-level factors are predictive of the police response. This is not surprising as it is indicative of the larger problem of how sexual assault is addressed by the public, the media and the criminal justice system.

We must consider the full range of difficulties associated with the criminal justice processing of sexual assaults. Police must work within the context of the larger criminal justice system and have no control over the behavior of prosecutors and other actors down the line. Recent research by Spohn and Tellis (2012) suggests that police and prosecutors are closely consulting about how to proceed in sexual assault cases. In some situations – police may be seeking input about the arrest decision regardless of whether they have probable cause (Pattavina, Morabito, and Williams 2016; Spohn and Tellis 2012). When a police officer believes that a case is unlikely to be prosecuted, he or she may attempt to convince the victim that it is not in her interest to pursue the case (Kerstetter 1990). Thus, it is important to enhance our understanding of how gender relates to the downstream orientation associated with sexual assault crimes. In addition, it would be helpful to consider measures of the gender diversity of prosecutors' offices given their hypothesized role in the decision-making process. This would allow us to see how that diversity relates to outcomes in these cases as the police and prosecution are clearly enmeshed in their decision-making.

Note

1. Budget was removed from the analyses because of multicollinearity problems. The correlation between budget and other independent variables was unacceptably high. There exists no other evidence of multicollinearity. Bivariate correlations and tolerance statistics indicate no other problems.

Disclosure statement

No potential conflict of interest was reported by the authors.

Funding

This work was supported by the National Institute of Justice [grant number 2012-IJ-CX-0052].

References

Alderden, M. A., and S. E. Ullman. 2012. "Gender Difference or Indifference? Detective Decision Making in Sexual Assault Cases." *Journal of Interpersonal Violence* 27 (1): 3–22.

Alexander, M. 2012. *The New Jim Crow: Mass Incarceration in the Age of Colorblindness*. New York: The New Press.

Archbold, C. A., and D. M. Schulz. 2008. "Making Rank: The Lingering Effects of Tokenism on Female Police Officers' Promotion Aspirations." *Police Quarterly* 11: 50–73.

Beichner, D., and C. Spohn. 2012. "Modeling the Effects of Victim Behavior and Moral Character on Prosecutors' Charging Decisions in Sexual Assault Cases." *Violence and Victims* 27 (1): 3–24.

Bouffard, J. A. 2000. "Predicting Type of Sexual Assault Case Closure from Victim, Suspect, and Case Characteristics." *Journal of Criminal Justice* 28 (6): 527–542.

Cordner, G., and A. Cordner. 2011. "Stuck on a Plateau? Obstacles to Recruitment, Selection, and Retention of Women Police." *Police Quarterly* 14: 207–226.

Doerner, W. M., and W. G. Doerner. 2010. "Collective Bargaining and Job Benefits: The Case of Florida Deputy Sheriffs." *Police Quarterly* 13 (4): 367–386.

Du Mont, J., K. L. Miller, and T. L. Myhr. 2003. "The Role of 'real rape' and 'real victim' Stereotypes in the Police Reporting Practices of Sexually Assaulted Women." *Violence against Women* 9 (4): 466–486.

Farrell, A. 2014. "Environmental and Institutional Influences on Police Agency Responses to Human Trafficking." *Police Quarterly* 17 (1): 3–29.

Farrell, Amy. 2015. "Explaining Leniency Organizational Predictors of the Differential Treatment of Men and Women in Traffic Stops." *Crime & Delinquency* 61 (4): 509–537.

Feeney, F. 2000. "Police Clearances: A Poor Way to Measure the Impact of Miranda on the Police." *Rutgers Law Journal* 32 (1): 1–57.

Garcia, V. 2003. "'Difference' in the Police Department: Women, Policing, and 'Doing Gender.'" *Journal of Contemporary Criminal Justice* 19: 330–344.

Haarr, R., and M. Morash. 1999. "Gender, Race, and Strategies of Coping with Occupational Stress in Policing." *Justice Quarterly* 16: 303–336.

UCR Handbook. 2004. "The Federal Bureau of Investigations (FBI)." Accessed at http://www.fbi.gov/ucr/handbook/ucrhandbook04.pdf

Heidensohn, F. 1992. *Women in Control? The Role of Women in Law Enforcement*. Oxford: Clarendon Press.

Jenness, V., and R. Grattet. 2005. "The Law-in-between: The Effects of Organizational Perviousness on the Policing of Hate Crime." *Social Problems* 52 (3): 337.

Jiao, A. Y. 2001. "Degrees of Urbanism and Police Orientations: Testing Preferences for Different Policing Approaches across Urban, Suburban, and Rural Areas." *Police Quarterly* 4 (3): 361–387.

Jordan, W. T., L. Fridell, D. Faggiani, and B. Kubu. 2009. "Attracting Females and Racial/Ethnic Minorities to Law Enforcement." *Journal of Criminal Justice* 37: 333–341.

Kennedy, B. 2012. "Unraveling Representative Bureaucracy: A Systematic Analysis of the Literature." *Administration & Society* 46: 395–421.

Kerstetter, W. A. 1990. "Gateway to Justice: Police and Prosecutorial Response to Sexual Assaults against Women." *Journal of Criminal Law & Criminology* 81: 267–313.

King, W. R. 2000. "Measuring Police Innovation: Issues and Measurement." *Policing: An International Journal of Police Strategies & Management* 23 (3): 303–317.

Krimmel, J. T., and P. E. Gormley. 2003. "Tokenism and Job Satisfaction for Policewomen." *American Journal of Criminal Justice* 28 (1): 73–88.

Lafree, G. D. 1989. "Official Reactions to Social Problems: Police Decisions in Sexual Assault Cases." *Social Problems* 582–594.

Langworthy, R. H. 1986. *The Structure of Police Organizations*, 132. New York: Praeger.

Leinen, S. 1984. *Black Police, White Society*. New York: NYU Press.

Logan, T. K., L. Evans, E. Stevenson, and C. E. Jordan. 2005. "Barriers to Services for Rural and Urban Survivors of Rape." *Journal of Interpersonal Violence* 20 (5): 591–616.

Maguire, E. R. 1997. "Structural Change in Large Municipal Police Organizations during the Community Policing Era." *Justice Quarterly* 14 (3): 547–576.

Maguire, E. R. 2003. *Organizational Structure in American Police Agencies: Context, Complexity, and Control*. Albany, NY: SUNY Press.

Maguire, E. R., J. B. Kuhns, C. D. Uchida, and S. M. Cox. 1997. "Patterns of Community Policing in Nonurban America." *Journal of Research in Crime and Delinquency* 34 (3): 368–394.

Martin, S. E. 1994. "'Outsider within' the Station House: The Impact of Race and Gender on Black Women Police." *Social Problems* 41: 383–400.

Mehay, S. L., and R. A. Gonzalez. 1994. "District Elections and the Power of Municipal Employee Unions." *Journal of Labor Research* 15 (4): 387–402.

Meier, K. J., and J. Bohte. 2001. "Structure and Discretion: Missing Links in Representative Bureaucracy." *Journal of Public Administration Research and Theory* 11 (4): 455–470.

Meier, K. J., and J. Nicholson-Crotty. 2006. "Gender, Representative Bureaucracy, and Law Enforcement: The Case of Sexual Assault." *Public Administration Review* 66: 850–860.

Meier, K. J., and Joseph Stewart. 1992. "The Impact of Representative Bureaucracies: Educational Systems and Public Policies." *The American Review of Public Administration* 22 (3): 157–171.

Morabito, M. S. 2008. "The Adoption of Police Innovation: The Role of the Political Environment." *Policing: An International Journal of Police Strategies & Management* 31 (3): 466–484.

Morabito, M. S. 2010. "Understanding Community Policing as an Innovation: Patterns of Adoption." *Crime & Delinquency* 56 (4): 564–587.

Morabito, M. S. 2014. "American Police Unions: A Hindrance or Help to Innovation?" *International Journal of Public Administration* 37: 773–780.

Morabito, M., and T. O. C. Shelley. 2015. "Representative Bureaucracy: Understanding the Correlates of the Lagging Progress of Diversity in Policing." *Race and Justice* 5 (4): 330–355. doi:10.1177/2153368715575376.

Morash, M., and R. Haarr. 1995. "Gender, Workplace Problems, and Stress in Policing." *Justice Quarterly* 12: 113–140.

Mosher, F. 1982. *Democracy and the Public Service*. New York: Oxford University Press.

Oberfield, Z. W. 2014. *Becoming Bureaucrats: Socialization at the Front Lines of Government Service*. Philadelphia, PA: University of Pennsylvania Press.

Pattavina, A., M. S. Morabito, and L. M. Williams. 2016. Examining Connections between the Police and Prosecution in Sexual Assault Case Processing: Does the Use of Exceptional Clearance Facilitate a Downstream Orientation? *Victims and Offenders: Journal of Evidence-based Policies and Practices* 11 (2): 315–334.

Pitkin, H. F. 1967. *The Concept of Representation*. Berkeley: University of California Press.

Pitts, D. W. 2005. "Diversity, Representation, and Performance: Evidence about Race and Ethnicity in Public Organizations." *Journal of Public Administration Research and Theory* 15 (4): 615–631.

Rabe-Hemp, C. 2009. "POLICEwomen or PoliceWOMEN? Doing Gender and Police Work." *Feminist Criminology* 4: 114–129.

Reaves, B. 2010. *Local Police Departments, 2007*. Washington, DC: Bureau of Justice Statistics. http://www.bjs.gov/content/pub/pdf/lpd07.pdf.

Reilly, Steve. 2015. "Tens of Thousands of Rape Kits Go Untested across the USA." *USA Today*, July. http://www.usatoday.com/story/news/2015/07/16/untested-rape-kits-evidence-across-usa/29902199/.

Rennison, C. M., M. Dragiewicz, and W. S. DeKeseredy. 2013. "Context Matters: Violence against Women and Reporting to Police in Rural, Suburban and Urban Areas." *American Journal of Criminal Justice* 38 (1): 141–159.

Rich, K., and P. Seffrin. 2014. "Police Interviews of Sexual Assault Reporters: Do Attitudes Matter?" *Violence and Victims* 27 (2): 263–279.

Schuck, A. M., and C. Rabe-Hemp. 2014. "Citizen Complaints and Gender Diversity in Police Organisations." *Policing and Society* 1–16. doi:10.1080/10439463.2014.989161.

Shelley, T. O. C., M. S. Morabito, and J. Tobin-Gurley. 2011. "Gendered Institutions and Gender Roles: Understanding the Experiences of Women in Policing." *Criminal Justice Studies: A Critical Journal of Crime, Law and Society* 24 (4): 351–367.

Simpson, S. S., L. A. Bouffard, J. Garner, and L. Hickman. 2006. "The Influence of Legal Reform on the Probability of Arrest in Domestic Violence Cases." *Justice Quarterly* 23 (3): 297–316.

Smith, A. E., and K. R. Monaghan. 2013. "Some Ceilings Have More Cracks: Representative Bureaucracy in Federal Regulatory Agencies." *The American Review of Public Administration* 43: 50–71.

Sowa, Jessica E., and Sally Coleman Selden. 2003. "Administrative Discretion and Active Representation: An Expansion of the Theory of Representative Bureaucracy." *Public Administration Review* 63 (6): 700–710.

Spohn, C., and K. Tellis. 2012. "The Criminal Justice System's Response to Sexual Violence." *Violence against Women* 18 (2): 169–192. doi:10.1177/1077801212440020.

Stalans, L. J., and M. A. Finn. 2000. "Gender Differences in Officer's Perceptions and Decisions about Domestic Violence Cases." *Women & Criminal Justice* 11: 1–24.

Tasca, M., N. Rodriguez, C. Spohn, and M. P. Koss. 2012. "Police Decision Making in Sexual Assault Cases: Predictors of Suspect Identification and Arrest." *Journal of Interpersonal Violence* 28 (6): 1157–1177. doi:10.1177/0886260512468233.

Tellis, K. M., and C. C. Spohn. 2008. "The Sexual Stratification Hypothesis Revisited: Testing Assumptions about Simple Versus Aggravated Rape." *Journal of Criminal Justice* 36 (3): 252–261.

Theobald, Nick A., and Donald P. Haider-Markel. 2009. "Race, Bureaucracy, and Symbolic Representation: Interactions between Citizens and Police." *Journal of Public Administration Research and Theory* 19 (2): 409–426.

Van Riper, P. 1958. *History of the U.S. Civil Service*. Evanston, IL: Row Peterson and Company.

Walfield, S. M. 2016. "When a Cleared Rape is Not Cleared: A Multilevel Study of Arrest and Exceptional Clearance." *Journal of Interpersonal Violence* 31 (9): 1767–1792.

Walker, S. 1985. "Racial Minority and Female Employment in Policing: The Implications of 'Glacial' Change." *Crime and Delinquency* 31: 555–572.

Wilkins, V. M., and B. N. Williams. 2008. "Black or Blue: Racial Profiling and Representative Bureaucracy." *Public Administration Review* 68: 654–664.

Wilson, J. M. 2005. *Determinants of Community Policing: An Open Systems Model of Implementation*. Washington, DC: Rand Infrastructure, Safety, and Environment.

Winfree, L. T., Jr., and C. DeJong. 2015. "Police and the War on Women: A Gender-linked Examination behind and in Front of the Blue Curtain." *Women & Criminal Justice* 25 (1–2): 50–70.

Zhao, J., N. He, and N. Lovrich. 2005. "Predicting the Employment of Minority Officers in U.S. Cities: OLS Fixed-effect Panel Model Results for African American and Latino Officers for 1993, 1996, and 2000." *Journal of Criminal Justice* 33 (4): 377–386.

Examining the impact of organizational and individual characteristics on forensic scientists' job stress and satisfaction

Thomas J. Holt, Kristie R. Blevins and Ruth Waddell Smith

ABSTRACT

Research on job stress and satisfaction among police and correctional officers has dramatically improved our knowledge of the experiences of criminal justice system employees. There is, however, minimal research on the experiences of individuals whose work directly informs criminal justice practice, most notably forensic scientists who collect and analyze evidence in support of criminal investigations. This study is one of the first to address the gap in our knowledge using survey responses collected from a sample of 670 forensic scientists operating in local and state laboratories in 25 states across the US. Regression models demonstrate that scientists who report higher stress were females who worked more hours, who had a poor relationship with court actors, minimal managerial support, and role ambiguities that made it difficult to do their jobs. Those with greater job satisfaction were unmarried, highly educated individuals with positive attitudes toward their work, greater managerial support, and few problems concerning their roles in the workplace.

The tremendous increase in the capability and speed of evidence collection and scientific analysis changed the way that evidence is both perceived and used by personnel in the criminal justice system (National Academy of Sciences 2009; Peterson et al. 2010; Roman et al. 2008). Both law enforcement and prosecutors have placed increasing emphasis on the use of forensic evidence to identify offenders, support investigations, and facilitate successful prosecutions (Eisenstein and Jacob 1977; National Academy of Sciences 2009; Peterson et al. 2010).

The work tasks of scientists are often complex, requiring a high degree of technical training and continuing education (James, Nordby, and Bell 2009; National Academy of Sciences 2009). Furthermore, forensic scientists often operate within the militarized managerial and administrative structures of a police agency, though many are in unsworn positions, with co-workers from different backgrounds and education levels, working in disciplines with varying caseloads and demands on their time (James, Nordby, and Bell 2009; National Academy of Sciences 2009; Peterson et al. 2010). These pressures may create a stressful working environment for forensic scientists (Becker and Dale 2003; Peterson et al. 2010).

Research on the work responses of traditional law enforcement officers and criminal justice system employees demonstrates that individuals tend to experience high levels of stress, but also moderate to high levels of satisfaction (Alkus and Padesky 1983; Burke and Mikkelsen 2005; Dantzer 1987; Davidson and Veno 1980; Johnson et al. 2005) Work stress has been defined by the disconnect between job demands and employees' available resources and capabilities, with high levels leading to physical illness, psychological problems, wasting time or resources, absenteeism, burnout, and generally poor job performance (Anshel 2000; National Institute for Occupational Safety and Health 1999; Pflanz and Heidel 2003; Tang and Hammontree 1992). Work stress is also correlated with low levels of job satisfaction, as measured by the extent to which individuals feel fulfilled by, or otherwise enjoy their jobs (Castle and Martin 2006; Lambert 2004; Tewksbury and Higgins 2006).

Few studies have investigated the levels of stress and job satisfaction reported by forensic scientists within the criminal justice system despite their role in local or state police agencies and in courtroom proceedings to prosecute offenses (James, Nordby, and Bell 2009; National Academy of Sciences 2009; Peterson et al. 2010). It is likely that, as with other occupations, levels of job satisfaction and work-related stress may negatively impact job performance (Anshel 2000; Brough and Frame 2004; Israel et al. 1989; Marshall 2006; Mostert and Rothmann 2006; Newman and LeeAnne Rucker-Reed 2004; Tang and Hammontree 1992; Violanti et al. 2014). Thus, understanding the factors affecting occupational experiences can aid in the development of policies to reduce work stressors and improve general job performance (Anshel 2000; Brough and Frame 2004; Israel et al. 1989; Marshall 2006; Mostert and Rothmann 2006; Newman and LeeAnne Rucker-Reed 2004; Tang and Hammontree 1992; Violanti et al. 2014).

This exploratory study attempted to address the gap in the literature with a survey of forensic scientists ($n = 670$) working in the primary forensic disciplines in local and state law enforcement laboratories across the United States. The findings identify the individual and organization-level factors associated with higher levels of work stress and job satisfaction among forensic scientists. The implications of this study regarding forensic scientists' experiences and those of the larger criminal justice system are discussed in detail.

Research on the occupational reactions of criminal justice system employees

The role of forensic science in the criminal justice system has grown dramatically over the last few decades, becoming a key resource for prosecutors and police (Murphy 2007). Forensic laboratories may operate at the state or local level within police agencies, though many scientists are not sworn officers. Scientists also frequently engage with law enforcement officers and prosecutors, and encounter victims, offenders, and witnesses during courtroom testimony. As a result, forensic scientists play a crucial role in support of criminal justice system actions despite differences in the situational and contextual experiences they have in the course of their job compared to police, probation, and correctional officers.

The generally scant research on the field of forensics within criminal justice has focused on either laboratory directors' perceptions of scientists' stress (Becker and Dale 2003), or on the experiences of the specialized sub-discipline of digital forensics (Burns et al. 2008; Holt and Blevins 2011; Holt, Blevins, and Burruss 2012; Holt, Burruss, and Bossler 2015; Krause 2009; Perez et al. 2010; Stevenson 2007). There is limited knowledge concerning the experiences of individual forensic scientists working in the primary disciplines of biology, controlled substances, toxicology, trace evidence, firearms and toolmarks, and latent prints (James, Nordby, and Bell 2009; National Academy of Sciences 2009). The diversity of scientific disciplines operating within a laboratory environment coupled with police agencies and the criminal justice system create unique dynamics that shape the occupational experiences of scientists, and understanding their experiences may lead to policy implications that could be beneficial to both employees and employers.

Measuring scientists' levels of stress and satisfaction is vital for understanding the potential triggers for stress, and to identify policies and procedures that may minimize negative experiences and increase productivity (Abdollahi 2002; Patterson 1992). Given that forensic scientists engage with system actors, playing a role in the process of cases through the criminal justice system, and may be in the employ of police agencies, it is plausible that their occupational experiences may have some similarity to traditional police officers. This analysis will examine known correlates for job stress and satisfaction as identified in studies of police officers (e.g., Abdollahi 2002; Anshel 2000; Cullen et al. 1985) as a basis to understand their relationship to forensic scientists experiences.

Research on occupational responses has identified five organization-specific sources of stress affecting employees: (1) stressors intrinsic to the job, (2) relationships at work, (3) role within the organization, (4) career development, and (5) organizational structure and climate (Cooper and Marshall 1980; Johnson et al. 2005). With respect to stressors that are a function of the position, one key factor is a work overload as evident in the number of hours worked each week. The greater number of hours an individual works each week may generally be associated with higher levels of stress, particularly for those who work multiple overtime hours. There is some evidence that forensic scientists, particularly in state-run laboratories, are more likely to work more than 40 h per week with less flexibility in scheduled hours (Becker and Dale 2003). This workload may be a consequence of the large backlog of evidence that must be processed in support of certain cases, such as sexual assault kits. Such workload issues may not be equally distributed across all disciplines, though there is evidence that all disciplines report a greater number of working hours on the job (Becker and Dale 2003).

Another factor intrinsic to the job is the number of work tasks an individual must perform outside of his or her office or facility. Time spent in duties that extend an employee beyond the bounds of his or her usual workspace or intrude on personal time are also associated with stress (Hunnur, Bagali, and Sudarshan 2014). Forensic scientists have two unique sources of stress due to outside work tasks related to courts and prosecutors. First, scientists can be called to testify in court, which takes them out of the laboratory and requires coordination with their managers and prosecutors. Such a task may increase stress because of increased responsibility, or may increase satisfaction with their jobs as they are given the opportunity to directly engage with the judge and jury regarding their casework.

The relationship that a scientist has with prosecutors and other court actors may also be associated to increased stress and reduced job satisfaction. Specifically, scientists may be requested to rapidly process evidence for certain cases despite large backlogs or queues of pending cases, increasing stress levels. Similarly, the 'CSI effect,' resulting from the media's exaggerated presentations of the role of forensic evidence in criminal investigations, may lead forensic scientists to be pressured by court actors when there is an absence of support for claims made regarding evidence (e.g., Brewer and Ley 2010; Shelton 2008).

Work relationships are one of the primary factors associated with stress among criminal justice system employees, most notably from support from supervisors and management (Cullen et al. 1985; Grossi, Keil, and Vito 1996; Liou 1995; Van Voorhis et al. 1991). The bureaucratic and militarized structure of criminal justice agencies is known to place a substantial degree of stress on police and correctional officers (Coman and Evans 1991; Cullen et al. 1985; Martelli, Waters, and Martelli 1989). This is due in part to tight controls placed on officers by management, limiting the ability to fully exercise discretion in the field (Martelli, Waters, and Martelli 1989; Spielberger et al. 1981). Owing to this, officers can feel alienated by an inability to communicate their needs to management in productive ways (Golembiewski and Kim 1990). These issues may be exacerbated for forensic scientists as they are often not sworn officers, yet function within a militarized chain of command that may be foreign to those with no prior military or law enforcement experience.

The roles individuals take on within an organization are also key sources of stress, particularly in criminal justice occupations. Research among law enforcement officers indicates that they report high levels of stress due to substantive role conflicts or ambiguity, measured through competing demands and different or unclear standards for completing specific tasks (Cullen et al. 1985; Pogrebin 1978). This could also be true for forensic scientists as they regularly interact with laboratory managers, prosecutors, police, and other criminal justice system actors (Becker and Dale 2003, 2007). Each of these groups has its own interests and needs regarding evidence processing, which may increase the demands placed on scientists and raise their overall level of stress (Becker and Dale 2003, 2007; Gould and Leo 2010; Saks et al. 2003).

A lack of clear conduct guidelines for work tasks, often referred to as role ambiguity, decreases employee job satisfaction (Coman and Evans 1991; He, Zhao, and Archbold 2002; Symonds 1970). This has particular salience for forensic scientists as there is often no single, nationally standardized methodology for processing evidence and obtaining results within certain scientific disciplines (National Academy of Sciences 2009; Stevenson 2007). As a result, the presence of role ambiguity has the potential to increase their work stress and decrease job satisfaction.

Further, there is an association between correctional employees and those in the helping professions' attitudes about their jobs and their levels of both job satisfaction and job stress (Griffin et al. 2010; Koeske and Koeske 1993; Myhren, Ekeberg, and Stokland 2013; Sarmiento, Laschinger, and Iwasiw 2004; Um and Harrison 1998). Individuals with a positive outlook about their work and its impact on the community are more likely to report greater job satisfaction and reduced stress. Those with negative attitudes toward their job often have reduced satisfaction and greater stress, which could be a function of occupational burnout (Aziri 2011). Thus, there is a need to understand how attitudes toward a job influence occupational responses of forensic scientists.

Individual-level factors also directly influence the experience of stress. Multiple demographic factors are correlated with reported levels of stress and satisfaction among studies of criminal justice employees and the helping professions, which may also correspond to forensic scientists. These relationships are mixed, depending on the study and the sample population, making it difficult to identify clear patterns in some cases. For example, some studies have found that younger individuals experience more work stress and less job satisfaction (Patterson 2003; Violanti 1983), while others have found no relationship (Dowler 2005; Storch and Panzarella 1996).

There are also gender differences, particularly in criminal justice occupations, as female police and correctional officers report more work stress and lower levels of satisfaction than males (Belknap and Shelley 1993; Burke and Mikkelsen 2005; Krimmel and Gormley 2003; Morash, Haarr, and Kwak 2006; Zhao, Thurman, and He 1999). Race differences are also evident, with minorities reporting greater levels of stress and less satisfaction than whites (Dowler 2005; Haarr and Morash 1999; Violanti and Aron 1995; Zhao, Thurman, and He 1999). Similarly, marriage appears to reduce reported levels of stress due to the ability to use an existing support network to aid in stress relief (He, Zhao, and Archbold 2002).

There is mixed evidence of the influence of higher education on occupational responses among police and correctional officers (Cullen et al. 1985; Storch and Panzarella 1996). Cullen and associates (1985) suggested that higher levels of education are related to lower levels of work stress due to better coping mechanisms. The fact that forensic scientists in biology, chemistry, and other disciplines increasingly require graduate degrees may help to reduce stress (National Academy of Sciences 2009). Individuals with advanced degrees may also report higher job satisfaction because of their interest in the field.

The number of years an individual has spent in forensic science can affect levels of stress and satisfaction. The influence of occupational experience has been inconsistent in previous studies of law enforcement officers (Zhao, Thurman, and He 1999), with some reporting that more experienced officers have higher work stress and lower job satisfaction than inexperienced officers (Johnson et al. 2005; Zhao, Thurman, and He 1999). More experienced officers may gain additional job responsibilities over time, or alternatively, grow more cynical about their jobs. In contrast, more experienced officers may have less stress and more satisfaction because they are familiar and comfortable with their jobs (Hunt and McCadden 1985).

Data and methods

This study utilized a purposive quantitative research design to understand the factors that affect forensic scientists' occupational experiences, and the ways that their tasks are affected by various managerial, social, and environmental conditions. The research team distributed an initial email survey coordinated with the Executive Director and management of the American Society of Crime Laboratory Directors-Laboratory Accreditation Board (ASCLD-LAB), the entity that is responsible for accreditation of forensic laboratories. The Director's office distributed an email to the laboratory directors of all currently accredited laboratories. The email included a description of the project, informed consent for the study, and an electronic link to the survey instrument. The first solicitation was delivered on 2 November 2012, with a reminder message sent on 2 December 2012 to increase the overall response rate.

The electronic solicitation method yielded 568 responses, though there is no way to determine the response rate due to the distribution method. Though this creates a substantial limitation regarding the response rate, scientists from 31 states and the District of Columbia participated. Responses primarily came from scientists in state ($n = 313$), and local police agencies ($n = 121$), with substantially lower responses from federal ($n = 30$) and private ($n = 20$) laboratories. The distribution of responses is somewhat similar to the general distribution of laboratories accredited by ASCLD-LAB at that time (ASCLD-LAB 2013).

In order to increase the general representation of laboratories from across the country, a follow-up paper survey was distributed on 7 May 2013 to 84 agencies in 25 states that were under-represented in the electronic survey data. The team constructed a package that was mailed to the laboratory director of each facility along with an introductory letter explaining the reason for the mail and its contents. Packages included individually sealed envelopes to be distributed to each scientist working in the laboratory, which contained a consent document, paper survey, and self-addressed envelope to return the survey. Twenty agencies were excluded from the sample due to missing contact information and non-response as the team could not properly distribute survey materials to a specific point of contact within the agency.

A total of 1,569 surveys were mailed, and 331 surveys from 20 states were returned. The response rate for the paper survey distribution was 21.1%, which is consistent for general response rates for such a method (Dillman 2007). The majority of responses were again from scientists in state ($n = 184$) and local ($n = 52$) agencies, while six independent scientists and one federal laboratory employee responded.

The 2 survey methods resulted in a total of 899 responses from a range of laboratory types. In order to examine the occupational responses of scientists working most closely with the criminal justice system, only those respondents from state or local law enforcement laboratories were included. Federal and privately operated laboratory employees were excluded as they may experience different working conditions due to factors such as different regulations. State and local laboratories, however, generally operate under similar policies and guidelines (Siegel 2013). This reduced the final sample size to 670 scientists, limiting its general representation of all scientists within the field; however, there is virtually no research on forensic scientists working within criminal justice agencies. Thus, the responses from these individuals provide a valuable purposive, convenient sample to explore the experiences of forensic scientists, especially biologists and chemists, operating in local and state laboratories.[1]

Measures

Dependent variables

Indicators were derived from existing research on occupational stress and satisfaction of various criminal justice system employees and traditional occupations outside of this field (Cullen et al. 1985; Jackson and Maslach 1982; Quinn and Shepard 1974; Rizzo, House, and Lirtzman 1970). These items allow us to directly compare the experiences of forensic scientists to that of the larger body of criminal justice system employees (Table 1).

Specifically, occupational stress was measured using a five-item additive index ($\alpha = 0.860$) created using statements adapted from scales that have been successfully applied in previous research exploring occupational stress among criminal justice employees, as well as other occupations (e.g., Blevins et al. 2007; Cullen et al. 1985; Jex, Beehr, and Roberts 1992; Peters and O'Connor 1980). Respondents were presented with five statements and asked to indicate their agreement with each, using a six-item Likert scale ranging from strongly agree to strongly disagree. The statements included: (1) 'I usually feel that I am under a lot of pressure when I am at work'; (2) 'When I am at work, I often feel tense or uptight'; (3) 'I am usually calm and at ease when I am working'; (4) 'Working with difficult images/scenes/materials all day is a real strain for me'; and (5) 'I feel frustrated by my job'.[2] Each of the items in this scale are recoded

Table 1. Descriptive statistics.

	n	Valid %
Individual characteristics		
Sex		
Male	253	38.0
Female	413	62.0
Race		
White	614	92.9
Nonwhite	47	7.1
Married		
Yes	477	71.7
No	188	28.3
Education		
Two-year degree or less	40	6.0
Four-year degree	295	44.2
Some graduate classes	87	13.0
Master's degree	233	34.9
Doctoral degree	12	1.8
Years in forensic sciences		
Less than 1	15	2.3
1–5	164	24.8
6–10	192	29.0
11–15	115	17.4
More than 15	176	26.6

	Mean	Range	SD	Median
	n	Valid %		
Age	38.67	23–66	9.95	37.00
	n	Valid %		
Work-related variables				
Times testified in previous year				
0	148	22.1		
1–5	343	51.2		
6 or more	179	26.7		
	Mean	Range		
Hours worked per week	41.83	10–90	5.39	40.00
Prosecutor/court relationship scale	3.64	1.90–5.50	0.67	3.70
Supervisor support scale	4.19	1.17–6.00	0.98	4.50
Manager support scale	3.66	1.00–6.00	1.39	3.67
Role problems scale	3.12	1.00–6.00	0.93	3.00
Perception of the Job	4.37	1.00–6.00	0.87	4.33
	n	Valid %		
Outcome measures				
Work stress				
Low	121	21.6		
Medium	317	56.6		
High	122	21.8		
Job satisfaction				
Low	95	16.2		
Medium	177	30.2		
High	315	53.7		

general feelings of work stress, providing a broad perspective on the amount experienced by scientists. Responses were coded so that larger numbers indicated higher levels of stress.

Replies were added and averaged, then divided into an ordinal scale where (1) 1.0–2.4999 indicated low stress, (2) 2.5–4.4999 indicated moderate stress, and (3) 4.5–6.0 indicated high levels of stress.[3] Summary statistics of the dependent variables indicate that just over half (56.6%) the respondents reported moderate levels of work stress, while 21.6% reported low stress and 21.8% reported high levels of stress. Items measured with Likert scales are often treated as continuous, interval level variables even though they are measured at the ordinal level (Jamieson 2004). Depending on the situation, composite measures composed of Likert responses may be used appropriately at either level. Thus, the dependent variables, job stress and job satisfaction, were categorized and treated as ordinal for the purposes of this analysis to conduct a multivariate ordinal regression.

The measure for job satisfaction comprised an additive scale of five measures ($a = 0.826$) with specially designed Likert scale responses, which were drawn from the *Quality of Employment Survey* (Quinn and Shepard 1974) that has been successfully used in a wide range of criminal justice research (Blevins et al. 2007; Cullen et al. 1985; Van Voorhis et al. 1991). These measures included: (1) 'All in all, how satisfied are you with your job?'; (2) 'Knowing what you know now, if you had to decide all over again whether to take the job you now have, what would you decide?'; (3) 'In general, how well would you say your job measures up to the sort of job you wanted when you took it'; (4) 'If a good friend of yours told you he (or she) was interested in working in a job like yours for your employer, what would you tell them,'; and (5) 'If you were free to go into any type of job you wanted, what would your choice be?' This scale is intended to measure general feelings of job satisfaction rather than specific measures of satisfaction concerning items such as particular job duties, relationships with co-workers, and salary. Responses were coded so that larger values represented higher levels of job satisfaction, then placed in an ordinal scale in which (1) 1–2.4999 indicated low satisfaction, (2) 2.5–3.4999 indicated satisfaction, and (3) 3.5–5 indicated high levels of job satisfaction. More than half (53.7%) of the scientists were highly satisfied, while 30.2% were moderately satisfied, and 16.2% reported low job satisfaction.

Independent variables

Six independent variables were included to assess the relationship between individual-level factors and occupational responses. The age of respondent was included as a continuous variable, while sex was a binary measure (0 = male; 1 = female). A binary measure was also used for race (0 = nonwhite; 1 = white) and marital status (0 = no; 1 = yes) due to skewed responses to the broader response categories presented above. Education was measured through an eight-item response (1 = High school diploma; 2 = Some college experience; 3 = Two-year degree; 4 = Four-year degree; 5 = Some graduate classes; 6 = Master's degree; 7 = Doctoral Degree; 8 = Other). Finally, the respondent's years spent in forensic science was measured through a seven-item categorical variable based on years in the field (1 = less than 1 year; 2 = 1–5 years; 3 = 6–10 years; 4 = 11–15 years; 5 = 16–20 years; 6 = 21–25 years; 7 = 26 or more years).[4]

An additional set of six variables was created to assess the relationship between working experiences, stress, and satisfaction. First, the average number of working hours each week was measured using a continuous variable for time spent at work. Second, an additive scale was created for the respondent's relationship with prosecutors based on responses to 11 questions: (1) 'Prosecutors doubt my competence'; (2) 'Prosecutors do not understand why it takes time to complete the analyses they request'; (3) 'Prosecutors try to persuade me to testify to more than just the scientific facts'; (4) 'I am not often thanked by prosecutors or police for the work that I do'; (5) 'I find it easy to deal with court schedules across the jurisdiction(s)'; (6) 'Judges respect me professionally'; (7) 'Judges and juries are frequently confused when there is insufficient forensic evidence to support claims made by prosecutors or police'; (8) 'Prosecutors do not inform me about the outcomes of the cases on which I work'; (9) 'Most court decisions are too lenient'; (10) 'Prosecutors do not understand that I sometimes work very hard on a case even though I end up finding no evidence'; and (11) 'I am regularly pressured by police or prosecutors to rush to produce scientific results.' Possible scores on the composite measure ranged from one to six, with higher scores representing more positive relationships ($a = 0.776$).

Supervisory support was measured through work-related variables assessing the willingness of management to support or encourage employees in the course of their jobs, as well as to resolve disputes between co-workers (Cullen et al. 1989). Respondents were asked to rate their agreement with the following statements: (1) 'My immediate supervisor supports me'; (2) 'My immediate supervisor gives me clear instructions'; (3) 'My immediate supervisory has clear expectations of me'; (4) 'The people I work with often have the importance of their jobs stressed to them by their supervisors'; (5) 'My supervisor often encourages the people I work with if they do their job well.'; and (6) 'When my supervisors have a dispute with one of my fellow co-workers they usually try to handle it in a friendly way' ($\alpha = 0.832$).[5]

Top managerial support was measured through a three-item scale ($\alpha = 0.850$) measuring scientists' relationships to directors and/or management in their laboratory. Respondents were asked to rate their agreement with the following items: (1) 'The top managers in my agency are responsive to my thoughts and suggestions.'; (2) 'The top managers in my agency are mainly concerned with getting cases out the door.'; and (3) 'The top managers in my agency are more concerned with looking good to the public than doing a good job.' For each measure, items were coded so that higher scores indicate more support, with possible scores ranging from one to six.

A measure for role problems was created using five measures ($\alpha = 0.751$) taken directly from the well-tested Rizzo, House, and Lirtzman (1970) and Churchill et al. (1985) measures. These measures identify issues associated with role conflict, ambiguity, and overload. Each of the items is related to a lack of staff, lack of uniform or standardized methods to complete a task, an absence of clearly defined work responsibilities, or incompatible work requests. The five measures were: (1) 'I have to do things at work in ways that should otherwise be done differently.'; (2) 'I do things that are likely to be accepted by one person but not accepted by others.'; (3) 'At work I receive assignments without the manpower to complete them.'; (4) 'In my job, I receive incompatible requests from two or more people.'; and (5) 'I have adequate resources and materials to complete them [tasks/assignments].'

An additional item for general perceptions concerning the job itself was included in the analyses due to the inconsistent relationships noted between job satisfaction and potential feelings of burn-out in research on various occupations (Griffin et al. 2010; Koeske and Koeske 1993; Myhren, Ekeberg, and Stokland 2013; Sarmiento, Laschinger, and Iwasiw 2004; Um and Harrison 1998). Three measures were included to assess the perceptions scientists hold about their jobs. These included: (1) 'I feel I am positively influencing other people's lives through my work.'; (2) 'I feel exhilarated after working on a case.'; and (3) 'I have accomplished many worthwhile things in this job.' Responses ranged from one to six, with higher scores reflecting greater agreement with the statement. A scale was created from these three measures with higher scores representing more positive feelings overall ($\alpha = 0.704$).

Findings

Multivariate ordinal regression was used to investigate the effect of potentially significant individual characteristics and work-related variables found in the literature on the dependent variables.[6] Ordinal regression was selected as it is an extension of general linear model, utilizes an ordinal dependent variable, and provides estimations of the odds of experiencing certain levels of the dependent variable based on the independent variables included in the model (Norusis 2012). Table 2 contains the results of work stress regressed on the independent variables.[7] An examination of the predictive ability of the individual characteristics measured revealed that, although being married approached significance, sex was the only significant individual characteristic in the model. The odds of females falling in the high work stress category were 1.919 greater than males when all other variables in the model were held constant.

Most of the work-related variables were significant predictors of work stress. Only two predictors were not significant: the number of times respondents testified in court in the previous 12 months and the scale for general feelings about work. Results for the five significant work-related predictors revealed that respondents who had good relationships with prosecutors and courts, as well as those who perceived higher levels of support from supervisors and managers, had lower levels of work stress. Further, scientists who worked more hours per week and experienced higher levels of role problems reported higher levels of job-related stress. The amount of role problems experienced by respondents was especially important, as a single unit increase in the role problems scale increased the odds of experiencing high levels of work stress 3.022 times.

Table 2. Predictors of work stress by multivariate ordinal regression.

	Parameter estimate	Standard error	p	Exp(B)	95% CI
Individual characteristics					
Age	0.000	0.021	0.990	1.000	−0.041 to 0.040
Female	0.652	0.238	0.006	1.919	0.185 to 1.118
White	0.846	0.443	0.056	2.330	−0.023 to 1.715
Married	0.114	0.253	0.653	1.121	−0.382 to 610
Education	−0.069	0.094	0.463	0.933	−0.253 to 0.115
Years in forensic sciences	0.174	0.124	0.161	1.190	−0.069 to 0.417
Work-related variables					
Hours worked per week	0.053	0.020	0.009	1.054	0.013 to 0.093
Prosecutor/court relationship	−0.820	0.180	0.000	0.440	−1.174 to −0.467
Supervisor support scale	−0.498	0.129	0.000	0.608	−0.751 to −0.246
Manager support scale	−0.183	0.093	0.050	0.833	−0.366 to 0.000
Role problems scale	1.106	0.160	0.000	3.022	0.793 to 1.419
Times testified	0.268	0.166	0.107	1.307	−0.057 to 0.594
Perception of the job	−0.240	0.136	0.077	0.787	−0.506 to 0.026
Model information					
Chi-square = 261.800, sig. = 0.000					
Nagelkerke R^2 = 0.513					

Table 3. Predictors of job satisfaction by multivariate ordinal regression.

	Parameter estimate	Standard error	p	Exp(B)	95% CI
Individual characteristics					
Age	−0.028	0.020	0.174	0.972	−0.067 to 0.012
Female	0.046	0.233	0.843	1.047	−0.411 to 0.504
White	−0.389	0.430	0.365	0.678	−1.232 to 0.453
Married	−0.492	0.249	0.048	0.611	−0.980 to −0.005
Education	0.201	0.096	0.037	1.223	0.012 to 0.389
Years in forensic sciences	−0.012	0.124	0.920	0.988	−0.255 to 0.230
Work-related variables					
Hours worked per week	−0.037	0.020	0.067	1.038	−0.077 to 0.003
Prosecutor/court relationship	0.080	0.168	0.635	1.083	−0.250 to 0.409
Supervisor support scale	0.650	0.124	0.000	1.916	0.407 to 0.893
Manager support scale	0.230	0.089	0.010	1.259	0.055 to 0.405
Role problems scale	−0.464	0.140	0.001	0.629	−0.738 to −0.189
Times testified	0.341	0.166	0.040	1.406	0.016 to 0.666
Perception of the job	1.080	0.141	0.000	2.945	0.803 to 1.357
Model information					
Chi-Square = 222.910, sig. = 0.000					
Nagelkerke R^2 = 0.457					

Findings for the job satisfaction model are presented in Table 3.[8] Two individual characteristics emerged as significant predictors of levels of job satisfaction. Specifically, married respondents were 0.611 times less likely to experience a high level of job satisfaction than those who were not married. Scientists with higher levels of education were more likely to experience greater levels of job satisfaction. Age, sex, race, and years worked in the field were not significant predictors of job satisfaction.

Five of the work-related variables were significant in the job satisfaction model (Table 3). As with the stress model, role problems and perceived levels of support from both supervisors and managers were important in predicting satisfaction. As hypothesized, respondents with less role problems and those with more perceived support from superiors experienced greater levels of job satisfaction. The odds of experiencing high levels of job satisfaction increased for each one unit change in the number of times a respondent testified in court during the previous year (1.406) as well as their positive perceptions of the job (2.945).

Discussion and conclusions

As forensic science plays an increasingly prominent role in legal investigations and court proceedings, the demands on laboratory scientists have grown substantially (Becker and Dale 2003; Durose et al. 2008; National Academy of Sciences 2009; Peterson and Hickman 2005; Peterson et al. 2010). The decreasing funds in local and state budgets limit the ability of forensic laboratories to maintain a sufficient number of scientists who can meet the requests and needs of prosecutors and police (Durose et al. 2008; National Academy of Sciences 2009; Peterson et al. 2010). As a consequence, these conditions may directly affect the occupational experiences of scientists by increasing work stress and decreasing general levels of job satisfaction (Anshel 2000; Becker and Dale 2003; Donald et al. 2005; Newman and LeeAnne Rucker-Reed 2004). To expand on the scant research in this area, this study measured the prevalence of stress, satisfaction, and prospective stressors through a broad survey of forensic scientists across the US.

The scientists in this sample reported moderate levels of work stress, and slightly higher levels of occupational satisfaction than those reported by other criminal justice employees (Abdollahi 2002; Anshel, Robertson, and Caputi 1997; Blevins et al. 2007; Burke and Mikkelsen 2005; Cullen et al. 1985; Holt and Blevins 2011; Holt, Blevins, and Burruss 2012; Kirkcaldy, Brown, and Cooper 1998; Patterson 2003), and helping professions (Nathan et al. 2007; Sterud et al. 2007; Webb, Sweet, and Pretty 2002). In addition, a substantial proportion of respondents felt they had good working relationships with the court system and had good managerial support within their workplace.

Analysis of the occupational factors associated with greater levels of stress and satisfaction demonstrated that scientists working a greater number of hours each week reported greater levels of stress. Thus, there is a need for careful consideration of scheduling to minimize negative work experiences. Higher levels of stress were also associated with a lack of support from supervisors, management, and court actors, and those with support were more likely to be satisfied with the job. The presence of role conflict, ambiguity, and other role problems increased the likelihood of work stress and decreased occupational satisfaction due to the lack of consistent standards for analysis and reporting (see also Coman and Evans 1991; He, Zhao, and Archbold 2002; Hepburn and Albonetti 1980; Symonds 1970).

There were some differences in the predictors of job satisfaction, suggesting stress and satisfaction are different constructs. Specifically, scientists who testified more often were more likely to report job satisfaction. The experience of sharing knowledge and professional opinions, as well as playing a public and direct role in a criminal case, may enhance a scientists' perception of the value of their work. In much the same way, respondents who feel good about their jobs were more likely to be satisfied. Scientists who recognize that their work has a beneficial impact and actually enjoy the process of the job are more likely to feel satisfied by their role in the workforce.

The only individual characteristics associated with satisfaction and stress were somewhat consistent with prior research. In addition, females were almost two times more likely to report more job stress than their male counterparts. This finding is consistent with previous research on police officers (Burke and Mikkelsen 2005; Krimmel and Gormley 2003; Morash, Haarr, and Kwak 2006; Zhao, Thurman, and He 1999), but it is not clear why females in this sample reported more stress than males. The relationship identified may stem from differences in the experiences of unsworn females working in a quasi-military structure where more males are in sworn positions, particularly in supervisory roles. Scientists who were married were less likely to report satisfaction, which may stem from negative impacts on their relationship due to job demands and long working hours. This finding is in contrast to research on policing which finds that marriage reduces stress among officers (He, Zhao, and Archbold 2002). As a result, there is a need for additional research exploring the relationship between sex and occupational experiences in the field as a whole.

The analyses presented here suggest that forensic scientists share many common occupational experiences with employees of the larger criminal justice system. Work-related variables are extremely important in predicting levels of work stress and satisfaction. Agencies and managers must develop policies focused toward addressing organizational factors that negatively impact occupational reactions. First, managers should consider ways to minimize the number of overtime hours scientists work each week. This may not be immediately possible if scientists must work more than 40 h each week to decrease case backlogs or because of mandates by state budgets and a lack of trained staff to more evenly distribute hours (Becker and Dale 2003; Fairbrother and Warn 2003; National Institute for Occupational Safety and Health 1999). There may be inherent value in either developing equitable distributions of overtime hours across scientists within a given area, or developing flex hours or shifts that are more convenient for scientists working extensive overtime. Allowing scientists to exercise some control over their scheduling during periods of high overtime could provide mechanisms to manage demands from their home and personal lives, making them more satisfied and reducing stress.

Second, the relationship between scientists' work reactions and their perceptions of supervisory and top management support indicates the need for well-defined policies and open lines of communication. Establishing clear lines of communication both up and down the chain of command can give scientists direct access to upper management, and foster trust between all parties (Becker and Dale 2003). The use of open staff meetings where management is present may also help to increase communications between scientists and management, and generally promote support for the scientific staff.

Third, laboratory management could benefit from carefully written policies concerning exact procedures for specific laboratory processes and staffing plans to reduce any redundancies in personnel and diminish the likelihood of role conflicts or uncertainty concerning responsibilities. Clear expectations and procedures for employees can lower individual levels of stress and increase job satisfaction by ensuring that individual work roles are understood and achieved on a daily basis. Similarly, scientists experiencing negative relationships with prosecutors and courts were significantly more likely to report job stress. Management may benefit from workplace policies that are clearly communicated to all partner agencies served by their scientists, including identifying requirements for the time needed to process evidence and appropriate avenues for contact with scientists. Overall, this may improve the occupational experiences of scientists, and help to solidify managerial support of scientists in their labs.

Though this study provides initial insights into the occupational responses of bench scientists across the various forensic disciplines, there are a number of limitations that must be addressed in future research. Scientists from most forensic disciplines and regions of the US participated in this study, though it may under-represent the larger field of forensic science generally as there is no way to determine the overall response rate who participated. Future studies must develop more robust and representative populations of scientists across the country, particularly in local laboratories, in order to better understand the experiences of forensic scientists generally.

There is also a need for research to understand why there are unusually few demographic factors associated with occupational stress and satisfaction among forensic scientists. Significant differences in the experiences of police officers on the basis of race, age, and gender have been identified in previous research on policing (Burke and Mikkelsen 2005; Krimmel and Gormley 2003; Lim and Teo 1998; Morash, Haarr, and Kwak 2006; Zhao, Thurman, and He 1999), and the lack of significance for age, race, years in the occupation, and education for forensic scientists is an interesting divergence from existing research on criminal justice system employees (Folkman et al. 1987; Patterson 2003; Violanti 1983).

There is no immediate explanation for these findings, and it has been proposed that age and other personal factors influence the ways that individuals cope with their occupations (Folkman et al. 1987). Other individual attributes, such as personality types, should also be explored. There is evidence that personality is related to occupational reactions (Jex 1992), and personalities of forensic scientists might be related to stress and/or satisfaction directly or indirectly through particular tasks, such as testifying in court. There is also a need for research considering the relationship between the specific scientific discipline a scientist works within and their occupational reactions as certain fields may be more heavily tasked on a day-to-day basis. For instance, biology and chemistry often have large case backlogs which require substantial scientist time, leading to grant programs to help offset costs from additional man-hours (Bettinger-Lopez 2016). Such research may help improve our understanding of the unique situational factors affecting scientists beyond organizational or individual characteristics.

There is also a need for further study exploring the ways that law enforcement and prosecutors perceive the role of forensic science generally. The results of this analysis suggest that the working relationships that scientists have with other criminal justice system employees and the requests they make affect their work experiences. There has been little research examining the ways that these agencies consider their impact and relationship to the forensic sciences (Peterson et al. 2010). Exploring these relationships could improve our knowledge of the complexities of the interactions between the various components of the criminal justice system and the forensic sciences, and find strategies to improve the function and experiences of all facets of the justice system process.

Notes

1. A comparison of the various populations sampled may be instructive to understand differences in the experiences of scientists working in private laboratories relative to public-funded agencies. This is, however, beyond the scope of this study and its focus on those scientists working most closely with the criminal justice system.
2. The measures in the occupational stress scale used here replicate those used in most research on criminal justice system employees. Organizational psychology prefers to use only the three measures specifically related to stress rather than including items that may otherwise be conflated with measures of individual burnout. To ensure the validity of the measure used, a factor analysis was conducted using oblique rotation which found that all five items loaded onto a single construct. Furthermore, all composite measures presented throughout this analysis loaded on to a single factor, except supervisory support which is discussed separately.
3. Given the distribution of the two dependent variables, equal-width binning was used to identify the high and low categories rather than a single summative scale (see Kotsiantis and Kanellopoulos 2006). Remaining values composed the moderate category.
4. Years spent in forensic science was measured as a categorical variable in the survey rather than an open-ended continuous measure in order to simplify the question for respondents, and is in keeping with other measures used in analyses of stress and satisfaction generally (e.g., Cullen et al. 1985; Holt and Blevins 2011).
5. A factor analysis was conducted to assess whether these items all load onto a single measure. The results suggest a two-factor solution, though the second factor consisted of only one measure: the people I work with often have the importance of their job stressed to them by their supervisors. The findings in the regression models were consistent whether or not this item was used in the supervisory support scale. Ultimately, the item was left in the composite measure because of the stable results and the frequent use of this item in supervisory support scales in the larger literature.
6. The largest variance inflation factor was 2.619 for the stress model and 2.263 for the satisfaction mode, indicating that multicollinearity was not a problem for either model. The multivariate ordinal regression assumption of proportional odds was confirmed by the non-significant test of parallel lines for each model.
7. Separate regression models were created to examine the influence of only individual characteristics and only work-related variables on stress. The combined model was the best fit (pseudo $R^2 = 0.029$ for individual characteristics and 0.480 for work-related variables).
8. Separate models were created to regress job satisfaction on only individual characteristics and only work-related variables. The combined model was the best fit (pseudo $R^2 = 0.015$ for individual characteristics and 0.422 for work-related variables).

Acknowledgments

The points of view or opinions expressed in this study are those of the authors and do not necessarily reflect the opinions of the National Institute of Justice or the US Department of Justice.

Disclosure statement

No potential conflict of interest was reported by the authors.

Funding

This work was supported by the National Institute of Justice, US Department of Justice [grant number 2011-DN-BX-0006].

References

Abdollahi, M. Katherine. 2002. "Understanding Police Stress Research." *Journal of Forensic Psychology Practice* 2: 1–24.

Alkus, Stephen, and Christine Padesky. 1983. "Special Problems of Police Officers: Stress-related Issues and Interventions." *The Counseling Psychologist* 11: 55–64.

American Society of Crime Laboratory Directors Laboratory Accreditation Board. 2013. *ASCLD/LAB Accredited Laboratories.* January 25, 2013. http://www.ascld-lab.org/labstatus/accreditedlabs.html.

Anshel, Mark H. 2000. "A Conceptual Model and Implications for Coping with Stressful Events in Police Work." *Criminal Justice and Behavior* 27: 375–400.

Anshel, Mark H., Michelle Robertson, and Peter Caputi. 1997. "Sources of Acute Stress and Their Appraisals and Reappraisals among Australian Police as a Function of Previous Experience." *Journal of Occupational and Organizational Psychology* 70: 337–356.

Aziri, Brikend. 2011. "Job Stress: A Literature Review." *Management Research and Practice* 3: 77–86.

Becker, Wendy S., and W. Mark Dale. 2003. "Strategic Human Resource Management in the Forensic Science Laboratory." *Forensic Science Communications* 5. https://www.fbi.gov/about-us/lab/forensic-science-communications/fsc/oct2003/index.htm/2003_10_research01.htm.

Becker, Wendy S., and W. Mark Dale. 2007. *The Crime Scene: How Forensic Science Works.* New York: Kaplan.

Belknap, Joanne, and Jill Kastens Shelley. 1993. "The New Lone Ranger: Policewomen on Patrol." *The American Journal of Police* 12: 47–60.

Bettinger-Lopez, Carrie. 2016. "The Sexual Assault Kit Initiative: An Important Step Toward Ending the Rape Kit Backlog." The White House Blog. Accessed March 15. https://www.whitehouse.gov/blog/2016/03/15/sexual-assault-kit-initiative-important-step-toward-ending-rape-kit-backlog

Blevins, Kristie R., Francis T. Cullen, James Frank, Jody L. Sundt, and Stephen T. Holmes. 2007. "Stress and Satisfaction among Juvenile Correctional Workers: A Test of Competing Models." *Journal of Offender Rehabilitation* 44: 55–79.

Brewer, Paul R., and Barbara L. Ley. 2010. "Media Use and Public Perceptions of DNA Evidence." *Science Communication* 32: 93–117.

Brough, Paula, and Rachael Frame. 2004. "Predicting Police Job Satisfaction Intentions: The Role of Social Support and Police Organizational Variables." *New Zealand Journal of Psychology* 33: 8–16.

Burke, Ronald J., and Aslaug Mikkelsen. 2005. "Gender Issues in Policing: Do They Matter?" *Women in Management Review* 20: 133–143.

Burns, Carolyn M., Jeff Morley, Richard Bradshaw, and Jose Domene. 2008. "The Emotional Impact on and Coping Strategies Employed by Police Teams Investigating Internet Child Exploitation." *Traumatology* 14: 20–31.

Castle, Tammy L., and Jamie S. Martin. 2006. "Occupational Hazard: Predictors of Stress among Jail Correctional Officers." *American Journal of Criminal Justice* 31: 65–80.

Churchill, Gilbert A., Jr., Neil M. Ford, Steven W. Hartley, and Orville C. Walker Jr. 1985. "The Determinants of Salesperson Performance: A Meta-analysis." *Journal of Marketing Research* 22: 103–118.

Coman, Greg, and Barry Evans. 1991. "Stressors Facing Australian Police in the 1990s." *Police Studies* 14: 153–165.

Cooper, Cary L., and Judi Marshall. 1980. *White Collar and Professional Stress.* New York: Wiley.

Cullen, Francis T., Terrence Lemming, Bruce G. Link, and John F. Wozniak. 1985. "The Impact of Social Supports on Police Stress." *Criminology* 23: 503–522.

Cullen, Francis T., Faith E. Lutze, Bruce G. Link, and Nancy Travis Wolfe. 1989. "The Correctional Orientation of Prison Guards: Do Officers Support Rehabilitation?" *Federal Probation* 53: 33–42.

Dantzer, Mark L. 1987. "Police-related Stress: A Critique for Future Research." *Journal of Police Criminal Psychology* 44: 1–7.

Davidson, Marilyn J., and Arthur Veno. 1980. "Stress and the Policeman." In *White Collar and Professional Stress*, edited by Cary L. Cooper and Judi Marshall, 131–166. New York: Wiley.

Dillman, Don A. 2007. *Mail and Internet Surveys: The Tailored Design Method*. Hoboken, NJ: Wiley.

Donald, Ian, Paul Taylor, Sheena Johnson, Cary Cooper, Susan Cartwright, and Susannah Robertson. 2005. "Work Environments, Stress, and Productivity: An Examination Using ASSET." *International Journal of Stress Management* 12: 409–423.

Dowler, Kenneth. 2005. "Job Satisfaction, Burnout, and Perception of Unfair Treatment: The Relationship between Race and Police Work." *Police Quarterly* 8: 476–489.

Durose, Matthew, R. Kelly, A. Walsh, and Andrea M. Burch. 2008. *Census of Publicly Funded Forensic Crime Laboratories, 2005*. Washington, DC: Bureau of Justice Statistics.

Eisenstein, James, and Herbert Jacob. 1977. Felony Justice: An Organizational Analysis of Criminal Courts. Boston, MA: Little Brown and Company.

Fairbrother, Kery, and James Warn. 2003. "Workplace Dimensions, Stress, and Job Satisfaction." *Journal of Managerial Psychology* 18: 8–21.

Folkman, Susan, Richard S. Lazarus, Scott Pimley, and Jill Novacek. 1987. "Age Differences in Stress and Coping Processes." *Psychology and Aging* 2: 171–184.

Golembiewski, Robert T., and Byong-Seob Kim. 1990. "Burnout in Police Work: Stressors, Strain, and the Phase Model." *Police Studies* 13: 74–80.

Gould, Jon B., and Richard A. Leo. 2010. "One Hundred Years Later: Wrongful Convictions after a Century of Research." *Journal of Criminal Law and Criminology* 100: 2010–2028.

Griffin, Marie L., Nancy L. Hogan, Eric G. Lambert, Kasey A. Tucker-Gail, and David N. Baker. 2010. "Job Involvement, Job Stress, Job Satisfaction, and Organizational Commitment and the Burnout of Correctional Staff." *Criminal Justice and Behavior* 37: 239–255.

Grossi, Elizabeth L., Thoomas J. Keil, and Gennaro F. Vito. 1996. "Surviving 'The Joint': Mitigating Factors of Correctional Officer Stress." *Journal of Crime and Justice* 19: 103–120.

Haarr, Robin N., and Merry Morash. 1999. "Gender, Race, and Strategies of Coping with Occupational Stress in Policing." *Justice Quarterly* 16: 303–336.

He, Ni, Jihong Zhao, and Carol A. Archbold. 2002. "Gender and Police Stress." *Policing: An International Journal of Police Strategies & Management* 25: 687–708.

Hepburn, John R., and Celesta Albonetti. 1980. "Role Conflict in Correctional Institutions." *Criminology* 17: 445–460.

Holt, Thomas J., and Kristie R. Blevins. 2011. "Examining Job Stress and Satisfaction among Digital Forensic Examiners." *Journal of Contemporary Criminal Justice* 27: 124–140.

Holt, Thomas J., Kristie R. Blevins, and George W. Burruss. 2012. "Examining the Stress, Satisfaction, and Experiences of Computer Crime Examiners." *Journal of Crime and Justice* 35: 35–52.

Holt, Thomas J., George W. Burruss, and Adam M. Bossler. 2015. *Policing Cybercrime and Cyberterror*. Durham, NC: Carolina Academic Press.

Hunnur, Rashmi R., Mettu M. Bagali, and Sudi Sudarshan. 2014. "Cause and Effect of Workplace Stress among Police: An Empirical Study." *International Journal of Management Research and Business Strategies* 3: 198–208.

Hunt, Raymond G., and Karen S. McCadden. 1985. "A Survey of Work Attitudes of Police Officers: Commitment and Satisfaction." *Police Studies* 8: 17–25.

Israel, Barbara A., James S. House, Susan J. Schurman, Catherine A. Heaney, and Richard P. Mero. 1989. "The Relation of Personal Resources, Participation, Influence, Interpersonal Relationships and Coping Strategies to Occupational Stress, Job Strains and Health: A Multivariate Analysis." *Work and Stress* 3: 163–194.

Jackson, Susan E., and Christina Maslach. 1982. "After-effects of Job-related Stress: Families as Victims." *Journal of Organizational Behavior* 3: 63–77.

James, Stuart H., Jon J. Nordby, and Suzanne Bell. 2009. *Forensic Science: An Introduction to Scientific and Investigative Techniques*. Florence, KY: CRC Press.

Jamieson, Susan. 2004. "Likert Scales: How to (Ab)Use Them." *Medical Education* 38: 1217–1218.

Jex, Steve M. 1992. *Stress and Job Performance: Theory, Research, and Implications for Managerial Practice*. Thousand Oaks, CA: Sage.

Jex, Steve M., Terry A. Beehr, and Cathlyn K. Roberts. 1992. "The Meaning of Occupational Stress Items to Survey Respondents." *Journal of Applied Psychology* 77: 623–628.

Johnson, Sheena, Cary Cooper, Sue Cartwright, Ian Donald, Paul Taylor, and Claire Millet. 2005. "The Experience of Work-Related Stress across Occupations." *Journal of Managerial Psychology* 20: 178-187.

Kirkcaldy, Bruce, Jennifer Brown, and Cary L. Cooper. 1998. "The Demographics of Occupational Stress among Police Superintendents." *Journal of Managerial Psychology* 13: 90–101.

Koeske, Gary F., and Randi D. Koeske. 1993. "A Preliminary Test of a Stress–Strain-Outcome Model for Reconceptualizing the Burnout Phenomenon." *Journal of Social Service Research* 17: 107–135.

Kotsiantis, Sotiris, and Dimitris Kanellopoulos. 2006. "Discretization Techniques: A Recent Survey." *International Transactions on Computer Science and Engineering* 32: 47–58.

Krause, Meredith. 2009. "Identifying and Managing Stress in Child Pornography and Child Exploitation Investigators." *Journal of Police and Criminal Psychology* 24: 22–29.

Krimmel, John T., and Paula E. Gormley. 2003. "Tokenism and Job Satisfaction for Policewomen." *American Journal of Criminal Justice* 28: 73–88.

Lambert, Eric G. 2004. "The Impact of Job Characteristics on Correctional Staff Members." *The Prison Journal* 84: 207–277.

Lim, Vivien K. G., and Thompson S. H. Teo. 1998. "Effects of Individual Characteristics on Police Officers' Work-related Attitudes." *Journal of Managerial Psychology* 13: 334–342.

Liou, Koutsai Tom. 1995. "Role Stress and Job Stress among Detention Care Workers." *Criminal Justice and Behavior* 22: 425–436.

Marshall, Katherine. 2006. "On Sick Leave." *Perspectives on Labor and Income* 18: 14–22.

Martelli, Theresa A., L. K. Waters, and Josephine Martelli. 1989. "The Police Stress Survey: Reliability and Relation to Job Satisfaction and Organizational Commitment." *Psychological Reports* 64: 267–273.

Morash, Merry, Robin Haarr, and Dae-Hoon Kwak. 2006. "Multilevel Influences on Police Stress." *Journal of Contemporary Criminal Justice* 22: 26–43.

Mostert, Karina, and Sebastian Rothmann. 2006. "Work-related Well-being in the South African Police Service." *Journal of Criminal Justice* 34: 479-491.

Murphy, Erin. 2007. "The New Forensics: Criminal Justice, False Certainty, and the Second Generation of Scientific Evidence." *California Law Review* 95: 721–797.

Myhren, Hilde, Øivind Ekeberg, and Olav Stokland. 2013. "Job Satisfaction and Burnout among Intensive Care Unit Nurses and Physicians." *Critical Care Research and Practice* 13: 1–6.

Nathan, Rajan, Andrew Brown, Karen Redhead, Gill Holt, and Jonathan Hill. 2007. "Staff Responses to the Therapeutic Environment: A Prospective Study Comparing Burnout among Nurses Working on Male and Female Wards in a Medium Secure Unit." *Journal of Forensic Psychiatry and Psychology* 18: 342–352.

National Academy of Sciences. 2009. *Strengthening Forensic Science in the United States: A Path Forward*. Washington, DC: Committee on Identifying the Needs of the Forensic Sciences Community; Committee on Applied and Theoretical Statistics, National Research Council.

National Institute for Occupational Safety and Health. 1999. *Stress…at Work*. Washington, DC: U.S. Department of Health and Human Services, Centers for Disease Control and Prevention.

Newman, Deborah Wilkins, and M. LeeAnne Rucker-Reed. 2004. "Police Stress, State-trait Anxiety, and Stressors among U.S. Marshals." *Journal of Criminal Justice* 32: 631–641.

Norusis, Marija J. 2012. *IBM SPSS Statistics 19: Advanced Statistical Procedures Companion*. New York: Pearson.

Patterson, Bernie L. 1992. "Job Experience and Perceived Job Stress among Police, Correctional, and Probation/Parole Officers" *Criminal Justice and Behavior* 19: 260–285.

Patterson, George T. 2003. "Examining the Effects of Coping and Social Support on Work and Life Stress among Police Officers." *Journal of Criminal Justice* 31: 215–226.

Perez, Lisa M., Jeremy Jones, David R. Englert, and Daniel Sachau. 2010. "Secondary Traumatic Stress and Burnout among Law Enforcement Investigators Exposed to Disturbing Media Images." *Journal of Police and Criminal Psychology* 25: 113–124.

Peters, Lawrence H., and Edward T. O'Connor. 1980. "Situational Constraints and Work Outcomes: The Influences of a Frequently Overlooked Construct." *Academy of Management Review* 5: 391–397.

Peterson, Joseph L., and Matthew J. Hickman. 2005. *Census of Publicly Funded Forensic Crime Laboratories 2002*. Bureau of Justice Statistics Bulletin. Washington, DC: US Department of Justice.

Peterson, Joseph, Ira Sommers, Deborah Baskin, and Donald Johnson. 2010. *The Role and Impact of Forensic Evidence in the Criminal Justice Process*. Washington, DC: National Institute of Justice.

Pflanz, Steven, and Stephen H. Heidel. 2003. "Psychiatric Causes of Workplace Problems." In *Mental Health and Productivity in the Workplace: A Handbook for Organizations and Clinicians*, edited by Jeffrety P. Kahn and Alan M. Langlieb, 276–296. San Francisco, CA: Jossey-Bass.

Pogrebin, Mark. 1978. "Role Conflict among Correctional Officers in Treatment Oriented Correctional Institutions." *International Journal of Offender Therapy and Comparative Criminology* 22: 149–155.

Quinn, Robert P., and Linda J. Shepard. 1974. *The 1972–1973 Quality of Employment Survey*. Ann Arbor: University of Michigan Survey Research Center, Institute of Social Research.

Rizzo, John R., Robert J. House, and Sidney I. Lirtzman. 1970. "Role Conflict and Ambiguity in Complex Organizations." *Administrative Science Quarterly* 15: 150–163.

Roman, John K., Shannon Reid, Jay Reid, Aaron Chalfin, William Adams, Carly Knight, and Justice Policy Center. 2008. *The DNA Field Experiment: Cost-effectiveness Analysis of the Use of DNA in the Investigation of High-volume Crimes*. Washington, DC: U.S. Department of Justice.

Saks, Michael J., D. Risinger, Robert Rosenthal, and William C. Thompson. 2003. "Context Effects in Forensic Science: A Review and Application of the Science of Science to Crime Laboratory Practice in the United States." *Science and Justice* 43: 77–90.

Sarmiento, Teresa P., Heather K. SPence Laschinger, and Carrol Iwasiw. 2004. "Nurse Educators' Workplace Empowerment, Burnout, and Job Satisfaction: Testing Kanter's Theory." *Journal of Advanced Nursing* 46: 134–143.

Shelton, Donald E. 2008. "The 'CSI Effect': Does It Really Exist?" *NIJ Journal* 259. Accessed December 1, 2015. http://www.nij.gov/journals/259/pages/csi-effect.aspx

Siegel, Jay A. 2013. "Criteria and Concepts for a Model Forensic Science Laboratory." *Forensic Science Policy & Management: An International Journal* 4: 23–28.

Spielberger, C. D., L. G. Westberry, K. S. Grier, and G. Greenfield. 1981. *The Police Stress Survey: Sources of Stress in Law Enforcement*. Washington, DC: Office of Criminal Justice Education, U.S. Department of Justice.

Sterud, Tom, Erlend Hem, Øivind Ekeberg, and Bjorn Lau. 2007. "Occupational Stress and Alcohol Use: A Study of Two Nationwide Samples of Operational Police and Ambulance, Personnel in Norway." *Journal of Studies on Alcohol and Drugs* 68: 896–904.

Stevenson, Jane. 2007. "Welfare Considerations for Supervisors Managing Child Sexual Abuse Online Units." Unpublished doctoral dissertation, Middlesex University, London, UK.

Storch, Jerome E., and Robert Panzarella. 1996. "Police Stress: State-trait Anxiety in Relation to Occupational and Personal Stressors." *Journal of Criminal Justice* 24: 99–107.

Symonds, Martin. 1970. "Emotional Hazards of Police Work." *The American Journal of Psychoanalysis* 30: 155–160.

Tang, Thomas Li-Ping, and Monty L. Hammontree. 1992. "The Effects of Hardiness, Police Stress, and Life Stress on Police Officers' Illness and Absenteeism." *Public Personnel Management* 21: 493–510.

Tewksbury, Richard, and George E. Higgins. 2006. "Examining the Effect of Emotional Dissonance on Work Stress and Satisfaction with Supervisors among Correctional Staff." *Criminal Justice Policy Review* 17: 290–301.

Um, Myung-Yong, and Dianne F. Harrison. 1998. "Role Stressors, Burnout, Mediators, and Job Satisfaction: A Stress–Strain-Outcome Model and an Empirical Test." *Social Work Research* 22: 100–115.

Van Voorhis, Patricia, Francis T. Cullen, Bruce G. Link, and Nancy Travis Wolfe. 1991. "The Impact of Race and Gender on Correctional Officers' Orientation to the Integrated Environment." *Journal of Research in Crime and Delinquency* 28: 472–500.

Violanti, John M. 1983. "Stress Patterns in Police Work: A Longitudinal Analysis." *Journal of Police Science and Administration* 11: 211–216.

Violanti, John M., and Fred Aron. 1995. "Police Stressors: Variations in Perception among Police Personnel." *Journal of Criminal Justice* 23: 287–294.

Violanti, John M., Anna Mnatskanova, Andrew Michael Hartley, Tara Fekedulegn Desta, Penelope Baughman, and Cecil Burchfiel. 2014. "Associations of Stress, Anxiety, and Resiliency in Police Work." *Occupational and Environmental Medicine* 7: 37–48.

Webb, D. A., D. Sweet, and I. A. Pretty. 2002. "The Emotional and Psychological Impact of Mass Casualty Incidents on Forensic Odontologists." *Journal of Forensic Sciences* 47: 539–541.

Zhao, Jihong, Quint Thurman, and Ni He. 1999. "Sources of Job Satisfaction among Police Officers: A Test of Demographic and Work Environment Models." *Justice Quarterly* 16: 153–173.

Gun crime incident reviews as a strategy for enhancing problem solving and information sharing

Natalie Kroovand Hipple, Edmund F. McGarrell, Mallory O'Brien and Beth M. Huebner

ABSTRACT

Over the last several decades, police departments and other criminal justice agencies have seen a shift toward a proactive problem-solving response to crime problems. This problem-solving orientation has often included an emphasis on expanded partnerships across criminal justice agencies as well as with a variety of community stakeholders, including researchers. This manuscript uses the issue of gun violence as a lens through which to examine the organizational and inter-organizational changes necessary to apply a data-driven, proactive, and strategic policing-led response to gun homicides and non-fatal shootings in four Midwestern sites. Each site adapted a unique data collection process and incident review. The data collection, incident reviews, and the varying models developed across the four cities, provide a reflection on corresponding organizational and inter-organizational changes that illuminate the movement toward this proactive, data-driven, problem-solving model of criminal justice. Fulfilling the promise of the incident reviews, however, requires internal organizational and cross-agency inter-organizational collaboration to align people, systems, and resources with this proactive, problem-solving model. Additionally, effectively implementing these organizational and inter-organizational changes appears dependent on commitment and leadership, collaboration and partnerships, data quality and availability, and training and communication within and across organizational boundaries.

Over the last several decades, police departments and other criminal justice agencies have seen a shift toward a proactive problem-solving response to crime problems. This problem-solving orientation has often included an emphasis on expanded partnerships across criminal justice agencies as well as with a variety of community stakeholders, including researchers (Roehl et al. 2008). Indeed, several scholars witnessing these trends labeled this the 'new criminal justice' and have argued that the criminal justice system's response to crime is no longer a simple reactive and linear process of case processing from police to courts to corrections (Klofas, Natalie, and Edmund 2010). Rather, the police are increasingly working with coalitions of agencies and organizations that pool their powers to serve crime reduction goals, are concentrating on fundamentally local problems and issues, and are increasingly data-driven and research based. And, for many reasons, local law enforcement most often must be the leaders in strategic responses to crime problems.

Although these shifts are not uniform across cities or criminal justice agencies, there are abundant signs of an increasing emphasis on goals and methods that emphasize a more proactive and problem-solving mission. These include studies of the impact of problem-solving initiatives focused on policing (e.g., Braga and Weisburd 2010), community supervision (e.g., Hawken and Kleiman 2009), and specialized courts (e.g., Mitchell et al. 2012b; Sevigny, Fuleihan, and Ferdik 2013). And, while there is great variation, there is evidence that proactive initiatives can reduce crime and criminal involvement. Traditionally, this research has focused on the outcomes of crime interventions, and researchers have yet to describe in detail the organizational processes needed to adopt these models, particularly using an organizational theory lens. This paper seeks to contribute to our knowledge about the efficacy of the problem-solving model in policing by examining one type of process focused on one specific problem in four distinct jurisdictions.

Specifically, this manuscript uses the issue of gun violence as a lens through which to examine the organizational and inter-organizational changes necessary to apply a data-driven, proactive, and strategic policing-led response to gun homicides (GH) and non-fatal shootings (NFS). This multi-jurisdictional case study (Creswell 2012) focuses on an innovative process for studying gun violence across four cities with medium to high levels of gun violence. Specifically, the manuscript will describe the innovative implementation of crime incident reviews (Klofas et al. 2006) spearheaded by local police departments to address gun-related crime. Data come from four cities: Detroit, Indianapolis, Milwaukee, and St. Louis. Although the implementation goals were the same, each site adapted a unique data collection process and incident review process (three sites). The data collection, incident reviews, and the varying models developed across the four cities, provide a reflection on corresponding organizational and inter-organizational changes that illuminate the movement toward this proactive, data-driven, problem-solving model of criminal justice.

Background and related research

Problem-solving movement

In the late 1970s, Herman Goldstein called for a fundamental shift in how the police think about their response to crime (Goldstein 1979, 1990). Rather than general strategies (e.g., randomized patrol) and a focus on responding to crime incidents (e.g., enhanced response times, clearance rates), Goldstein argued that the police needed to think about addressing specific categories of problems. Building on research demonstrating recurring patterns of different crime types (e.g., business burglaries during nighttime in contrast to daytime burglaries of residences; intimate partner violence in contrast to assaults in bars and taverns), the problem-solving model emphasized that crime prevention and control would be advanced much more effectively by improving responses to *problem types* as opposed to improved processing of individual cases. With the introduction of tools like the SARA (Scanning, Analysis, Response, and Assessment) Model (Eck and Spelman 1987), individual police officers were empowered to problem solve on their own. Using four steps, the SARA model helped guide police to identify problems, determine their underlying causes, and implement and assess evidence-based responses to those problems.

It appears that research on the problem-solving model itself has largely occurred in the context of policing. And, although research demonstrates promise across the problem-solving initiatives (Braga 2008; Braga and Weisburd 2010; Hawken and Kleiman 2009; Henry and Kralstein 2011; Mitchell et al. 2012a; Sevigny, Fuleihan, and Ferdik 2013), at least in the context of policing there is also evidence that problem-solving models like the SARA model are not always implemented as intended. For example, Cordner and Biebel (2005) studied problem solving in the San Diego Police Department, considered leaders in problem-solving policing, and found a significant gap between the 'Goldstein' model and the actual practice of problem solving (see also Braga and Weisburd 2006; Capowich and Roehl 1994; Tilley 1999). Specifically, there was a tendency to focus on individual problems (a problem person or a problem place) as opposed to groupings of problem types spanning blocks, neighborhoods, or a police beat. They also found that the analysis of the problem and impact assessment was often very limited. And, despite having an established crime analysis unit, there appeared to be limited involvement of crime analysts in the problem-solving efforts. There was also tendency to focus on drug and disorder problems to the exclusion of problems associated with property and violent crimes. That is, officers believed problem-solving policing was most effective when applied to less serious or 'soft' crimes such as drug and disorder problems and was not really applicable to all crimes, especially serious crime. Cordner and Biebel (2005) found a reasonably high level of support for problem solving but there was variation among officers consistent with other research that has found that problem solving may be limited to particular officers or units (Cordner and Biebel 2005; Skogan et al. 1999; Toch and Grant 1991).

In the context of the present research on gun crime, the problem-solving efforts move beyond individual officers to multiple units within the police department working in partnership with other criminal justice agencies. Additionally, the limitations of traditional police data sources for studying gun crime requires that the problem-solving analysis consider innovative approaches to analyzing the gun crime problem. Absent such innovation and organizational adaptations, problem analysis will be based on limited and selective incidents (e.g., homicides) and on limited information about the people, groups, places, and contexts of the incidents.

Organizational and inter-organizational dimensions

Problem-solving approaches in policing, prosecution, judicial and corrections contexts include internal organizational changes as well as collaboration across organizations. At the organizational level, the police have traditionally responded to calls for service, investigated alleged crimes, and made arrests tied to specific incidents. Prosecutors screen arrests and determine whether there is sufficient evidence to prosecute. The courtroom workgroup (prosecution, defense, judges, and court staff) handles specific cases to determine guilt or innocence and allocate sentences. Corrections staff then handle the individual offender according to the terms of his or her sentence (community sanctions, supervision, and/or incarceration). As such, criminal justice personnel who have traditionally worked as part of 'people processing' organizations (Hasenfeld 1972; Hasenfeld and Cheung 1985) responding to specific incidents, cases, and defendants, are now being asked to address persistent problems. This requires changes in orientation, work processes, communication patterns, and measures of organizational success.

As with all public bureaucracies, criminal justice agencies tend to resist change (Allen 2002; Miller, Ohlin, and Coates 1977) and thus the move toward a problem-solving model is not automatic and implementation is likely to be a challenge (Skogan and Hartnett 1997). As mentioned earlier, despite a long-term commitment to problem solving including training, organizational incentives, a robust crime analysis unit, and a data system for documenting problem-solving activities, San Diego is an example of the difficulty of implementing a different way of doing business (Cordner and Biebel 2005) (see also Skogan et al. 1999; Toch and Grant 1991).[1] This organizational resistance is compounded by the reality that all the affected organizations retain responsibility to their own day-to-day missions, to respond to calls from the public, and to process individual cases.

Incident reviews

Systematic incident reviews, typically focused on homicides, have developed as an approach to fill the gap in traditional information systems. Gun crime incident reviews build upon processes developed in public health. Specifically, public health researchers have utilized systematic mortality incident reviews to advance knowledge and improve practice in relation to fetal, infant, child, and maternal deaths (Hutchins, Grason, and Handler 2004). The public health reviews were developed to address limitations in the scope and timeliness of existing data systems. The reviews seek 'to improve the understanding of personal, social, and community as well as medical factors associated with adverse reproductive and infant health outcomes at the local level' (Hutchins, Grason, and Handler 2004, 259).

Although problem solving generally, and incident reviews as an analytical component of problem solving, can logically occur within single organizations, experience suggests these initiatives often occur in an inter-organizational context (Azrael, Anthony, and Mallory 2013; Braga et al. 2001; Klofas et al. 2006). Typically, incident reviews are part of expanded inter-organizational linkages as the goal is to bring multiple perspectives and multiple sources of information to the review. With respect to policing, problem-solving efforts typically call for establishing partnerships with local residents and neighborhood associations, business owners, code enforcement, utilities, and social services. Ideally, incident reviews include a variety of agency stakeholders that may have 'touched' the individuals (suspects, victims) and the groups or networks connected to the incident, the location of the incident, or have more general insight into the nature of the problem. Thus, successfully implementing crime incident reviews involves securing the support and cooperation of multiple units within and across multiple agencies. Those involved believe these partnerships provide additional sources of information (e.g., probationer and parolee information) as well as additional resources for addressing recurring problems (e.g., focused prosecution, code enforcement, Crime Prevention Through Environmental Design [CPTED] strategies), Milwaukee.

The emphasis on inter-agency collaboration to support both problem solving and crime incident reviews suggests an increased 'coupling' of what is typically seen as a loosely coupled system (or non-system) (Duffee 1980; Wright 1981). That is, rather than simply moving cases along the various components of the criminal justice system, problem solving and crime incident reviews attempt to foster information sharing about recurring problems across multiple agencies and stakeholders. Ideally, the information sharing leads to deeper understanding of the drivers of the crime problem and improved responses in terms of crime prevention and public safety.

The Boston Gun Project provides the first documented example of systematic incident reviews used as a key analytic process in criminology (Braga et al. 2001). Also referred to as Boston Ceasefire, this multi-agency initiative partnered criminal justice personnel with a research team that followed a problem-solving model that included systematic incident reviews of gun homicides involving youths. The incident reviews led to new insights about the nature of youth gun violence in Boston. Specifically, gun crime was highly concentrated among a small proportion of the youth population, victims and suspects overlapped across a number of dimensions, and youths involved in violent street groups were at considerably heightened risk for offending and victimization (Braga et al. 2001). These characteristics became the emphasis of the Boston Ceasefire focused deterrence intervention.

The success of Boston Ceasefire led to the adoption of systematic incident reviews in a series of similar problem-solving violence prevention and control initiatives including the Strategic Approaches to Community Safety Initiative (SACSI) (Roehl et al. 2008) and Project Safe Neighborhoods (PSN) (Klofas et al. 2006). The incident reviews sought to combine street-level intelligence from a variety of criminal justice sources to increase the understanding of the nature of gun crime and to inform local prevention and control strategies. That way, criminal justice officials could strategically focus limited resources for maximum effectiveness. Secondary benefits could include information to support investigations and clear cases and to identify system gaps or failures.

It is difficult, however, to analyze the impact of incident reviews because they are typically associated with specific interventions such as Boston Ceasefire, SACSI, or PSN (e.g., Braga et al. 2001; Klofas et al. 2006; McGarrell et al. 2006, 2010). An exception, however, is the evaluation of the Milwaukee Homicide Review Commission (Azrael, Anthony, and Mallory 2013). For purposes of the evaluation, the incident reviews focused on particular police districts (treatment sites) and found reductions in gun crime. Specifically, the treatment police districts observed over a 50 percent reduction in homicides that was statistically significant when compared to a nine percent reduction in the control districts (Azrael, Anthony, and Mallory 2013). Additionally, over a two and one-half year period, the Milwaukee Homicide Review Commission developed over 100 recommendations aimed at reducing homicides. These recommendations ranged from single agency recommendations such as recommending the police department increase patrols to problem taverns (reviews indicated 10 percent of homicides occurred in or directly outside a tavern) to co-locating Wisconsin Department of Corrections agents in the police district stations to allow for closer client supervision and improved police-agent collaboration. The Governor's Office funded this recommendation (O'Brien, Woods, and Cisler 2007).

Gun violence

In the instance of addressing gun crime, the lack of readily available data sources on gun crime incidents severely limits the ability of research to contribute to the understanding of gun violence and the development of evidence-based strategies for reducing gun violence. In 2005, the National Research Council's Committee on Law and Justice noted that information on gun-related violence was far too limited and fragmented to provide 'accurate, complete, timely, and detailed data on the incidence and characteristics of gun-related violence' (Wellford, Pepper, and Petrie 2005, 20). Historically, police incident data in the form of the Uniform Crime Reporting (UCR) system have provided descriptive data on gun crime limited largely to homicides. The Supplemental Homicide Reporting (SHR) system provides more details on homicides and both the SHRs and National Incident Based Reporting Systems (NIBRS) allow for the isolation of incidents involving guns. However, there is a considerable time delay before SHRs are available for analyses and NIBRS systems remain the exception rather than the rule for most jurisdictions in the United States as roughly one-third of law enforcement agencies participating in UCR reported via NIBRS in 2013 (Federal Bureau of Investigation 2015a). Even when focused on homicides in jurisdictions covered by SHR and NIBRS systems, researchers have questioned the reliability and validity of gun crime data elements such as victim-offender relationships and incident characteristics like gang involvement or intimate partner violence (e.g., Braga et al. 1999; Loftin 1986; Loftin et al. 2015; Maxfield 1989; Riedel 1990; Williams and Flewelling 1987). The additional limitation of the SHR's is the absence of data to study NFS.

The current study focuses on data collection and problem-solving efforts to better address gun violence through the use of systematic crime incident reviews. The study benefits by examining gun violence data collection and incident reviews efforts across four jurisdictions. Consequently, it provides the opportunity to examine similarities and differences across four jurisdictions, trade-offs associated with varying approaches to the incident reviews and their implementation, and consideration of the organizational and inter-organizational dimensions of systematic incident reviews as a component of problem solving.

The project

In 2014, the authors embarked on a 30-month project funded by the National Institute of Justice. The overarching goals of this project included both improvements in gun violence information systems as well as advancing basic knowledge about gun violence. Specific goals included: increasing understanding of the spatial and network dimensions of gun violence; creating a better understanding of NFS and how they relate to GH; and, improving data systems on gun violence. The research team proposed a 'ground-up' approach, working with four midwestern police departments to combine GH and NFS incidents into common databases and to supplement incident reports through a variety of data sources, with the main supplemental mechanism being crime incident reviews (Klofas et al. 2006). The initial project included Detroit, Indianapolis, and Milwaukee. St. Louis was added as the fourth site mid-way through the project and, while gun crime data collection was a priority in St. Louis, implementing crime incident reviews was not due to the shortened project time frame.

Table 1 displays the violent crime and homicide rates for the four study sites. Detroit and St. Louis are similar in their crime rates and are consistently ranked among the cities with the highest violent crime and homicide rates in the United States. Indianapolis and Milwaukee experience more moderate rates of violent crime, though both cities have rates over three times the national average for metropolitan jurisdictions.

Each site had a local research partner who was charged with data collection and coordinating and implementing crime incident reviews to fit the local context. The crime incident review process was

Table 1. Violent crime and homicides in project sites.

	Detroit	Indianapolis	Milwaukee	St. Louis	National Average MSA
2014 Violent Crime					
Total	13,616	10,768	8,864	5,348	
Rate per 100,000 people	1988.6	1254.7	1476.4	1678.7	395.7
Rank Order – Cities with more than 250,00 people	6	9	10	22	
2014 Homicide					
Total	298	136	86	159	
Rate per 100,000 people	43.5	15.8	15.0	49.9	4.7
Rank Order – Cities with more than 250,00 people	2	18	20	1	

Source: Federal Bureau of Investigation (2015b).

rooted in the Milwaukee Homicide Review Commission process (O'Brien, Woods, and Cisler 2007). And, as expected, each site had its own specific data collection and review methodology based on existing data systems and the wants and needs of the local police organization. The overarching research question of this study is to what extent can gun crime incident reviews contribute to our understanding of gun crime and contribute to problem-solving prevention initiatives? With this broad question in mind, the research questions informing the current analysis include:

RQ1: How have incident reviews developed in these jurisdictions?

RQ2: What are the similarities and differences across the three jurisdictions in the incident reviews?

RQ3: What are the relative advantages and disadvantages of these approaches to the incident reviews?

RQ4: What are the benefits and the challenges of the incident reviews?

RQ5: What are the implications for organizational and inter-organizational and implementation dimensions necessary for the effective use of gun crime incident reviews?

Findings

All four sites have similar, long histories of federally supported multi-agency crime reduction efforts including SACSI, PSN, and the Comprehensive Anti-Gang Initiative (CAGI). Milwaukee has been conducting homicide reviews since 2005. Indianapolis conducted incident reviews during the SACSI project but had since discontinued the reviews. Indianapolis re-instituted crime incident reviews in late 2012, around the same time that Detroit embarked on reviews. The incident reviews were an important component for the current project. Although St. Louis does not conduct homicide or NFS reviews specifically, there is a long history of CompStat within the St. Louis Police Department. Consequently, St. Louis offers a valuable contrast to the other three cities and is likely representative of major city police departments that has not yet begun a formal process for homicide or NFS incident reviews.

Incident review development

In three sites, the development of incident reviews coincided with data collection efforts. As expected, the police departments at each site collected and maintained robust data pertaining to GH and they were able to extract homicide information easily to provide to the researchers. These data included victim and offender information, and case details such as location and motive. In contrast, with the exception of Milwaukee, none of the sites could provide accurate data on NFS. Therefore, the priority became establishing a system for collecting data on NFS if there was not one. The incident review process would be part of this; however, due to the volume of NFS at each site, NFS reviews would serve to supplement a larger NFS data collection method.

Beginning in late November 2013, the 'Detroit Ceasefire' team began holding weekly incident reviews covering all gun crime incidents in two police precincts that had among the highest levels of gun crime in the city. The gun crime incident reviews were developed as part of a gun violence prevention initiative modeled on the problem-solving component of Boston Ceasefire. The Detroit Ceasefire team agreed to follow this model and to use systematic incident reviews of gun crime incidents as the key analytical component of its ongoing problem solving intended to identify the drivers of gun crime violence in the 5th and 9th Precincts. As was the case in Milwaukee, as a National Incident Based Reporting System (NIBRS) jurisdiction,[2] Detroit was able to query the DPD records management system to identify aggravated assaults with a gun involving an injury. However, in order to meet the goals of timely identification of all NFS, it was necessary for a member of the research team to manually read aggravated assaults, armed robberies, carjackings and other firearms-involved incidents in order to identify and accurately count NFS in a real-time environment.

Indianapolis reinstituted incident reviews in 2012 after years without them. Recognizing that NFS were approximately four times as common as GH, and noting the limited information available about NFS, a small multi-agency working group decided to attempt NFS incident reviews after a change in leadership. The reviews would supplement a citywide NFS data collection effort and review incidents would be a selection of NFS occurring in one zip code. This zip code was selected based on an analysis of historical criminal homicide data and the increased risk for young black males living in this geographic area to become a homicide victim. While there were no NFS data to supplement the homicide data at that time it was reasonable to assume that NFS would follow the same geographic and victim patterns.

Indianapolis does not proactively search police incident records management systems for NFS incidents. Instead, the research team is notified about NFS incidents via an internal police document that is completed by Aggravated Assault and Homicide detectives, usually within 24 h of a homicide or NFS. This internal document is the beginning point for data collection on all NFS. After receiving the internal document, the research team manually verifies all NFS like the other sites using available records management systems.

Milwaukee developed a multi-agency homicide review process in 2005, and PSN grant funds supported the first Milwaukee homicide reviews (http://city.milwaukee.gov/hrc). Initially the homicide reviews occurred in three of the seven police districts and then expanded citywide in 2008. In an effort to learn more about firearm violence, NFS associated with homicides were incorporated into the reviews in 2006. Milwaukee's commitment to NFS reviews was an extension of their long, uninterrupted commitment to homicide incident reviews. Milwaukee is similar to Detroit in that the research team proactively searches the police incident report records management system for NFS. In addition to verifying each incident, the research team also searches police calls for service data looking for incidents they might have missed.

This project allowed for some fine-tuning of the review process at each site. In Detroit, observations that many homicide and non-fatal shooting suspects and victims had prior carrying a concealed weapon (CCW) charges led to an expanded gun crime definition to include CCW arrests. Likewise, Indianapolis adjusted its NFS review case selection process several times since this project started. Each change was made to address 'missed' cases, which are cases participants felt were not being reviewed but should be.

And, most recently, Milwaukee, the site with crime incident reviews in place the longest, has changed the NFS reviews to focus on the most frequent perpetrators of gun violence and their associates. This change in case selection was intended not only to focus on the individuals most likely to be involved in gun violence but to also improve information sharing and intelligence on these individuals. Additionally, participation was expanded to include additional federal criminal justice partners (ATF, FBI).

Incident review structure

All four sites captured homicide and NFS data citywide but there were differences in the types of reviews conducted and how the reviews were structured (see Table 2). Milwaukee conducts both monthly homicide reviews focused on city-wide incidents and bi-weekly NFS reviews focused on a sample of NFS based on the meeting location (e.g., a meeting at the 3rd District police station focused on a sample NFS occurring in the 3rd district). NFS cases have been selected by the districts, investigation bureau, or by MHRC staff; criteria have varied from hotspots to gang-related to drug-related to robberies, the focus is driven by the stakeholders.

Indianapolis limited the focus of its monthly reviews to NFS using a triage approach to focus only on criminal NFS (accidental and self-inflicted NFS were excluded). In contrast to Milwaukee and Indianapolis, Detroit conducts weekly reviews focusing on all gun crimes in two contiguous police precincts. Gun crimes were defined to include homicides, non-fatal shootings, aggravated assaults with a firearm (i.e., shootings that did not result in a victim being struck; brandishing), armed robberies, and carjackings, and as noted earlier, CCW arrests. In essence, and consistent with the variation in geographic and crime focus, Detroit conducted weekly reviews with significantly more incidents while both Indianapolis and Milwaukee focused on a smaller number of incidents during monthly NFS reviews (Indianapolis), monthly homicide reviews, and bi-weekly NFS reviews (Milwaukee).

The distinctions also related to the preparation for the reviews. Given the bi-weekly or monthly frequency, Indianapolis and Milwaukee distributed case lists approximately one week before the review and prepared PowerPoint summaries to guide the review meeting. In Detroit, given the weekly frequency, the research team prepared case summaries and distributed them two days before the review. In Milwaukee and Indianapolis, police department officials provided case summaries and then the

Table 2. Project site summary.

	Detroit	Indianapolis	Milwaukee	St. Louis*
Crime incident review Geographic scope	2 precincts	City-wide	City-wide	City-wide
Gun homicide Data collection	City-wide	City-wide	City-wide	City-wide
Non-fatal shooting Data collection	City-wide	City-wide	City-wide	City-wide
Gun homicide Crime incident reviews	Yes	No	Yes- all homicides	-
Non-fatal shooting Crime incident reviews	Yes	Yes	Yes	-
Case selection for reviews	All GH and NFS cases occurring in 2 precincts	NFS – triage selection	GH – all NFS – triage selection	-
Meeting frequency	Weekly	Monthly	GH – Monthly NFS – Bi-weekly	-
Meeting length	90 min	2 h	2 h	-
Number of cases reviewed	20–25 gun incidents 3–6 CCW arrests	Up to 8 NFS	Up to 8 Homicides NFS – varies	-
Meeting preparation	Case summaries sent 2 days prior	Case list sent 1 week prior PowerPoint	GH– PowerPoint	-
Meeting Location	Police Department HQ	Police district HQ	GH – Department of Corrections NFS – Rotating district HQ	-
Case presentation	Precinct Lieutenant for case	Aggravated Assault/ Robbery Unit Ser- geant	GH- Homicide Unit Lieutenant NFS – District Per- sonnel	-

*St. Louis did not intend to implement gun crime incident reviews.

discussion was guided by the research team. In Detroit, officials from the police department guided the review discussions.

The reviews in the three sites were structured quite similarly in terms of participation And, while exact review attendees varied from meeting to meeting, by crime review type (GH or NFS), and by site, there were common partnerships represented across the three sites. Table 3 displays the partners who regularly and occasionally participated in reviews at each site. All three sites' reviews included representation of federal, state, and local partners. Although there were slight differences across the three sites, for example, Detroit and Milwaukee had more participation from federal law enforcement agencies, these variations tended to reflect differences in the structure of each organization. Occasional participation by some partners reflected both the cases being reviewed as well as resource availability. As expected, police department representation was significant at all sites. Table 3 also includes a more detailed list of police department attendees. All three sites included regular involvement from street-level officers and at least occasional involvement among command staff, homicide and/or major crimes investigators. Detroit and Indianapolis included special units such as gang and intelligence with Indianapolis also including the juvenile unit.

All three sites included local prosecutors as well as combinations of probation and parole, community corrections, and the Department of Corrections. Some of the local level variations included Detroit incorporating the state police, Indianapolis incorporating the crime lab, Milwaukee and Indianapolis occasionally incorporating jail staff, and both Indianapolis and Milwaukee including personnel from

Table 3. Agency review participation by site.

	Detroit	Indianapolis	Milwaukee
Federal Partners			
USAO	R		R
FBI	O		R
ATF	R		R
Probation	R	R	R
State Partners			
State Police	R		
DOC	R		R
Fusion Center		R	O
Local Partners			
Mayor's Office	R		
Police Department*	R	R	R
Prosecutor's Office	R	R	R
Sheriff's Office/Jail		O	O
Probation/Parole	R	R	R
Community Corrections	R	R	R
Crime Lab		R	
Nuisance Abatement		R	
School Police	O		R
Research Team	R	R	R
Civilian Coordinator	R		R
Outreach Coordinator	R		R
*Police Department Participants			
Command-level officers	R	O	O
Homicide Unit	O	R	R
Aggravated Assault/Robbery Unit		R	
Street-level/front line officers	R	R	R
Gang Unit	R	R	
Intelligence Unit	R	R	
Juvenile Unit		R	
Precinct-level special operations	R		R

Notes. R = Regular participation; O = Occasional participation.

fusion intelligence centers. Whereas Indianapolis included the juvenile unit from the lead police department (IMPD), both Detroit and Indianapolis included school police.

All three sites included research teams in the incident reviews. The teams consisted of a lead researcher affiliated with a local university and at least one research assistant. As noted earlier, the research team did considerable preparation for the reviews at each site. The research team also provided input and facilitated discussion as well as captured the data generated in the reviews. Follow-up questions were tailored to each site and their operational and data collection needs. For instance, Detroit had a specific interest in group and gang activity as it related to their gun crime incidents. Indianapolis tended to focus on repeat individuals (i.e., involved in multiple NFS in any role) and locations. Milwaukee often posed the question of whether anything could have been done to prevent the incident from occurring. Additionally, Detroit and Milwaukee included civilian project coordinators and outreach workers. In the case of Detroit, these were individuals responsible for Detroit Ceasefire whereas in Milwaukee these were individuals who were part of the Milwaukee Homicide Review Commission and employed by the Milwaukee Health Department, Office of Violence Prevention.

Benefits

As expected, there are advantages and disadvantages to the way in which each site conducted their reviews (see Table 4). As each site tailored their reviews to their local context, they had to take into consideration issues related to time sensitivity (i.e., operational and tactical responses), resource constraints (i.e., human and data), amount and detail of information related to gun crime (i.e., cross-district, cross-case). Thus, Indianapolis and Milwaukee prioritized strategic intelligence through less frequent but more comprehensive reviews of a smaller universe of incidents. Detroit prioritized tactical intelligence to support timely prevention actions through weekly reviews of a larger volume of incidents. The trade-off for Detroit was often very limited information about incidents whereas the trade-off for Indianapolis and Milwaukee was the potential loss of opportunity to intervene for prevention purposes. As time passed, each site adjusted its review structure as needed but involving trade-offs in the relative advantages and disadvantages summarized in Table 4.

The observed benefits of the incident reviews include those both internal and external to the police department. However, generally speaking, a benefit that affected the police department also carried external benefits to other participating agencies. For example, the reviews encouraged a significant change in communication and information sharing at all levels across all agencies. That is, all sites saw communication and information sharing benefits both intra- and inter-agency. And, in this context, 'information' could mean a wide variety of things. Certainly, information could include official data coming from agency records management systems. At the same time, information could also be lead information, information from a field notebook, or acquired from a citizen, unofficial in nature, and not recorded in any formal records management system.

The very nature of the multi-unit (i.e., within the police department) and multi-agency partnerships increased information sharing. The reviews served as a forum where units and officers who did not usually work side by side or regularly interact could share information about the gun crime incidents. The review meetings created the same opportunity for agencies across the state, local, and federal criminal justice system to share information with the local police department and other agencies. Agencies such as probation and parole could share information about the involvement of their clients and add to gang information from intelligence gathered in jails and prisons. State and federal prosecutors could glean information about cases they may decide warrant increased attention and consider the benefits of state vs. federal prosecution. They could also inform law enforcement partners about information they need to successfully prosecute cases. And, communication that occurred outside the reviews increased as well as a result of the relationships established through the review process.

Given the difficulty in collecting data specifically relating to NFS, the review process served as a good supplement to the data collection processes at all sites even though reviewing every gun crime incident or even just NFS in every city proved impossible. The crime incident reviews increased the strategic and

Table 4. Incident review dimensions.

Dimension		Advantages	Disadvantages
Geographic scope			
	Citywide	Comprehensive picture	Resource intensive
	Police district(s)	Easier to implement (resource-wise); Easier to tap into street-level knowledge	Limited generalizability; potential to miss cross-district elements
Crime scope			
	All gun crimes	Comprehensive picture; ability to observe escalation and connections across cases	Resource intensive
	Homicides & NFS	Ability to see connections across most serious gun violence	May miss patterns to other violent crime
	Homicide only	Easier to implement (resource-wise)	Miss majority of cases involving gun injury
	NFS only	Expands focus to all cases involving gun injury	May miss connections to homicides
Case selection			
	All GH and NFS	Opportunity to make connections across all cases	Time and resource intensive
	Triage selection	Time efficient	May miss cross-case connections
Meeting frequency			
	Weekly	Timely tactical information for intervening to prevent gun violence	Resource intensive; limited investigatory information
	Monthly	More detailed information from investigations and background information gathering	Limits ability for timely tactical prevention responses
Visual Aides			
	PowerPoint	Detail specific; can enhance discussion	Time and resource intensive

tactical understanding of gun violence at each site. For example, Detroit's reviews revealed that the proportion of gun violence attributable to violent street group members was smaller than observed in other cities that have deployed the Ceasefire strategy. In all three cities, the reviews have indicated that individuals involved in prior NFS as suspects, victims, and witnesses appear to be at high risk for future involvement in NFS and GH.

Creating a strategic understanding of gun violence helped inform tactical operations and resource deployment across sites. Review meetings often revealed immediate situations that could have resulted in further gun violence absent timely intervention by one of the participants such as retaliatory shootings against victims or witnesses. The reviews helped each site collect information specific to the local context and interest of the stakeholders (i.e., group and gang involvement, repeat individuals, prevention). Related, the incident reviews helped create a better understanding of the drivers of gun violence. This, in turn, created an environment that built shared commitment to addressing gun violence. While more difficult to quantify, accountability, coordination of efforts, cooperation, and service delivery all improved at the agency level. And, although cause and effect is difficult to disentangle, the simple act of meeting on a regular basis to review specific cases appeared to facilitate a shared commitment to addressing the lethal carnage discussed at each meeting.

Challenges

All four sites had long histories of actively working with researchers. As a result of this project, systematic gun crime data collection including NFS is occurring in all four sites and three of the four sites are conducting incident reviews. Collecting data and conducting reviews presented challenges, sometimes different, across the sites. Yet, while often time consuming, these challenges did not prove insurmountable for any of the sites and generally improved over time. Challenges to conducting gun crime incident reviews fell into three broad categories: people, systems, and resources.

People

Garnering support across multiple agencies to participate in the review process can be difficult. Commitment to the review process at the executive level was paramount not just for participation but for the required access to collect data and prepare for meetings. Concerns about resources, time commitment, and value of the reviews were constant for every agency. All sites reported an ebb and flow to the support for the review process and various challenges along the way related to gaining and maintaining support.

Engaging the right people to attend review meetings and bring available data were consistent challenges across sites. This was especially important as it related to the sharing of agency street-level information at meetings, that is, information not available in formal records management systems. And, as documented, the incident review process required heavy participation from law enforcement (Table 3). Often this required relying on specific officers (investigators, intelligence officers, etc.) to bring their knowledge and understanding of the individuals involved in the gun violence and the local context to the meetings. Meetings where 'key' individuals were not present often limited information sharing. Not having the right people at the meetings to respond to questions or act on the information presented often created frustration among partners because a primary goal of the meetings was to foster and identify opportunities for agency level action. For example, shared information about a problem house where the landlord seems unaware of the ongoing issues might create an opportunity for an invitation to landlord training or a mailed letter advising the landlord of the multiple police runs to the location. Similarly, information about an ongoing dispute involving dangerous individuals provides an opportunity for violence prevention but only if acted upon.

While staff turnover is quite common in police departments, it was exasperated by budget challenges, particularly in light of recent economic decline, and upper level staffing changes at all sites. Changes in administrations can both help and hurt project momentum. Staff changes resulted in frequent turnover among review meetings. Turnover also reduced the institutional knowledge of the process and, in some cases, lead to a decline in buy-in among key partners. The review staff repeatedly communicated the importance and value of the review process. Staff turnover at the ground level also made it more difficult to acquire street-level intelligence for the incident reviews. At the same time, there were instances of staff turnover that resulted in renewed commitment and enthusiasm for the review process.

And intertwined within all the people challenges is the issue of trust and personnel turnover created related challenges. As information sharing is the crux of the incident review meeting, participants must trust the others in the room in order to share information they would not normally share outside their own office workplace with people they would not normally share. Revealing details that are relevant to the review process but could also compromise a detective's case requires a significant amount of trust. Indeed, a 'visitor' to an incident review meeting could change the meeting dynamics enough to affect information sharing and effectively silence some participants. New participants may want to 'sit back and watch' for a few meetings before sharing information. Simple awareness of potential trust issues (see, for example, Braga and Hinkle 2010; Rojek, Martin, and Alpert 2015; Rojek, Smith, and Alpert 2012) as well as careful selection (or uninviting) of meeting participants is essential.

Systems

The review process was dependent on the access to data. Because the existing records systems at all four sites did not readily allow for extraction of NFS data and other non-GH crime, each had to create a mechanism to manually do this. Indeed, data collection of NFS proved to be equally challenging across all sites. As experience will support, figuring out how to collect accurate data that are not readily available electronically involves both art and science and each site accomplished this differently. Police departments are still the gatekeepers to the most informative data and each one is different. For this project, researchers needed access to more than just official records. And, it took time to get access, even with long time existing relationships in place. Each site had a research team, that is, not a single researcher, which usually meant records access was needed for more than one person. Background checks and in-depth screening were common and took time and resources.

Initially, the incident review process at each location led to frequent requests for 'new' information. For instance, discussions about an individual's criminal history might lead to a request for probation or parole status or perhaps incarceration history. These requests for additional information resulted in the identification of information gaps. In one site, the gang unit had been inactive for a period and gang intelligence was stored in paper format only. In another site, the criminal history database that the city had used for over 15 years was replaced by a new program that did not afford the same information in the same way. Data validity and reliability were questionable as the bugs were still being worked out in the new system.

And, in some cases, the data systems did not support questions that were being asked. For example, information about gang involvement or 'gang related' crime has proven difficult to capture system-atically and reliably across the sites. Information on disputes, which drive a lot of the gun violence (Wilson, MacDonald, and Tita 2010), is also hard to cull from police records management systems. Repeat individuals at different incidents, especially when not the victim or suspect, was important to review attendees but difficult to document outside of the reviews.

Related, sites encountered unexpected legal obstacles relating to the discussion and use of criminal history data for both adults and juveniles. In one case, it took about six months and a series of meetings to obtain formal permission to access and discuss records. In another site, the research team worked with team members to find a suitable substitution using police records management systems while working toward formal approval of state criminal history records. Finally, efforts are being made to increasingly utilize technologies such as National Integrated Ballistics Information Network (NIBIN) data and ShotSpotter data. However, in several sites, NIBIN is primarily used for forensics evidence as opposed to timely intelligence and ShotSpotter data are new or not available and therefore neither has enhanced the information sharing in the incident reviews.

Resources

Similar to the experience of police departments adopting Community-Oriented and Problem-Solving Policing (Greene 2004), attendees regularly had to balance every day demands like case investigations, court appearances, supervising clients, etc. with the time commitment of preparing for the reviews, attending the reviews, and acting upon the reviews. Police departments and partnering agencies con-sidering the costs and benefits of implementing reviews need to consider the resource demands.

The time to prepare for reviews varied across sites. Pre-meeting communications can be difficult given the number and variety of people involved and work schedules. As described above, all of three of the cities participating in the reviews benefited from the participation of research partners who helped prepare information for the reviews. Absent such research partners, crime analysts could play this role, although the neutrality afforded by the researcher would be lost. Some sites used PowerPoint presentations to help guide the meetings and discussion which required considerable time to prepare. Gathering, analyzing, and summarizing the information from reviews similarly involved an expenditure of human resources.

Finally, if the reviews are executed as they are intended, more often than not, they create more work for individuals and agencies through case follow-up and operationalization on information presented. Indeed, one of the observations across the three cities was that the perceived value of the reviews was often connected to the actionable intelligence generated therein. One telling example involved an automated teller machine (ATM) location that generated regular robberies, some of which included shootings. This pattern of offenses revealed in the reviews led to a lieutenant working with the bank that owned the ATM to limit the hours of operation with the goal of eliminating an apparent 'crime attractor' during high-risk periods. Although in the long-term this likely reduced calls for police service, in the short-term this required an additional set of responsibilities for this particular lieutenant. All of these activities (preparation, review, post-review actions), in turn, place pressure on people and systems in what are typically resource constrained environments.

Discussion

The incident reviews implemented in three of the study sites represented an innovative analytical approach to support problem-solving efforts intended to address the significant issue of gun violence. This study of the incident review process suggested that reviews represent a supplemental source of information to the picture of gun crime captured in police records management systems. Incident reviews have the potential of tapping into street-level intelligence existing within the police department as well as with other partnering organizations. This can increase the strategic understanding of gun violence, for example to what extent is gun violence being driven by gangs, disputes, intimate partner violence, drug markets, repeat locations, felons in possession of a firearm, or other factors? Correspondingly, incident reviews can increase the tactical understanding of current factors that may be driving violence such as active disputes among known groups; active chronic violent offenders; or incidents likely to generate retaliatory violence.

Achieving the promise of problem solving to address gun violence generally, or the goals of the incident reviews specifically, requires changes at the organizational and inter-organizational levels. Indeed, increased 'coupling' (Duffee 1980; Wright 1981) within and across organizations appears to be an important element of problem solving and incident reviews. This is reflected in the findings of the present study. In all three jurisdictions, the reviews brought together actors within the police department from various units and levels of the organization. Likewise, in all three sites the reviews involved collaboration, including police departments, state and/or federal law enforcement, prosecutors, corrections agencies, and other stakeholders. Rather than collaborating simply through the processing of cases, the reviews involved a common focus on problems, in this case gun crime.

The current study suggests that, similar to other criminal justice innovations (Feeley 1983; Rosenbaum 1986; Skogan and Hartnett 1997; Skogan et al. 1999), implementing crime incident reviews is difficult. Research indicates there are key dimensions that need to be present in order for successful implementation to occur (McGarrell and Hipple 2014) and this is likely to be the case for successful implementation of incident reviews. These dimensions include commitment and leadership, partnerships, data availability and sharing, and communication and training. Indeed, the importance of all four dimensions was evident in these three sites.

Commitment and leadership was critical for launching the incident reviews; for enlisting the participation of key people, units, and agencies; and for sustaining participation over time. In all three sites there were vacillations in participation but clear evidence that when key organizational leaders placed a priority on gun violence, problem solving, and the importance of the reviews, that the participation, preparation, sharing of information, and quality of information coming from the incident reviews was significantly enhanced. Similarly, all three sites experienced times when such commitment was not apparent and the reviews yielded more limited benefits.

The importance of the partnerships was also critical. As noted above, this involved people and the establishment of trust to share information openly in the inter-organizational context of the reviews. Partnerships were also affected by the commitment and leadership dimension as it was critical to have the right people from the partnering units and agencies bringing and sharing information.

McGarrell and Hipple (2014) posit that a core dimension of effective implementation of problem solving is the quality and access of data to support meaningful problem analysis. The incident reviews represented a concrete technique for expanding the ability to analyze gun crime. All four jurisdictions engaged in new efforts to collect information about NFS with the three jurisdictions implementing incident reviews seeking to add to the basic picture of gun violence found in police incident reports by tapping into street-level intelligence and multiple agency sources of information about the people, groups, places, and contexts driving gun crime.

One of the additional challenges of implementation mentioned by McGarrell and Hipple (2014), particularly when implementation is dependent on multiple units within an organization as well as inter-organizational partnerships, is the development of effective communication and training mechanisms. This related particularly to the 'people' challenges described earlier. Specifically, there was a need to create shared understanding of the purpose of the incident reviews, the dependency on preparation and participation by various actors involved in the reviews, and for sustaining this shared understanding in light of inevitable turnover.

In addition to continued study of these implementation dimensions, several additional research questions arose in this study. Whereas three of the four jurisdictions implemented crime incident reviews, each did so differently, tailoring them to their local context. This was reflected in the variations across the three jurisdictions on focal crimes (NFS, GH, all gun crime), geographic scope, all incidents versus select incidents, and similar elements. Although various advantages and disadvantages were apparent to the researchers (see Table 4), future research should address the trade-offs from the perspective of the participating agencies and the personnel involved in the reviews.

Moreover, a future goal of this research is to contrast the potential benefits of increased knowledge of patterns of gun violence yielded by incident reviews, weighing the concomitant costs and time requirements of this program, with data generated through existing information systems. Thus, St. Louis serves as a quasi-control site in the current analysis. From a theoretical perspective, the goal is to better understand if and how incident reviews offer unique insights into patterns of gun violence when compared to analyses of traditional police records management system. From a practical perspective, we hope to learn if the reviews generate tactical and strategic understanding of gun violence that can shape violence prevention and control strategies.

As noted at the beginning of this article, this project was funded by a grant from the National Institute of Justice. And, while all three sites implementing the reviews had initiated the reviews prior to the actual project period, grant funding supplemented the review process, made detailed data collection possible at all four sites, as well as funded research team involvement. It is impossible to ignore the role external funding plays in the development of multi-agency efforts like crime incident reviews and more broadly, police practitioner researcher partnerships (see, for example, Bales et al. 2014; Grieco, Vovak, and Lum 2014; Rojek, Smith, and Alpert 2012). This is not to say that incident reviews cannot be implemented without external or additional funding, rather, it makes it all the more important that the necessary organizational elements are in place for successful implementation and long-term sustainability (McGarrell and Hipple 2014).

Lastly, there is always the issue of sustainability of the data collection and review processes. Milwaukee has sustained the review process since inception in 2006. Detroit and Indianapolis have had periods of time with and without reviews occurring. St. Louis is still exploring the review process. The people, systems, and resources challenges presented here are both micro- and macro-level organizational issues that will most likely wax and wane over time and create difficulties not just for the review process itself but for overall sustainability. Maintaining support 'at the top' through political and departmental turnover is essential to sustainability. While the review process may continue during periods of less support, sites may not necessarily get what they need in terms of people, systems, and other resources. The need for financial support cannot be ignored. Sustainability discussions must include enhanced data collection methods and their automation which are expensive but must be weighed against declining resources to support sworn personnel. Both experienced sites and sites new to crime incident reviews must be vigilant and proactive in anticipating and responding to challenges related to sustainability.

Conclusion

This research suggests the promise of gun crime incident reviews for supporting problem-solving approaches to address the serious issue of gun violence. The expansion of incident reviews beyond homicides to include NFS, and in the case of Detroit additional gun crimes, significantly adds to the picture of gun violence and increases opportunities to identify the patterns of people, groups, places, and contexts driving gun violence in each of the cities. This contributes to the basic understanding of gun violence within each city and across cities, provides a strategic analysis to inform evidence-based prevention and control strategies, and offers tactical understanding for timely prevention and enforcement. Fulfilling the promise of the incident reviews, however, requires internal organizational and cross-agency inter-organizational collaboration to align people, systems, and resources with this proactive, problem-solving model.

Additionally, effectively implementing these organizational and inter-organizational changes appears dependent on commitment and leadership, collaboration and partnerships, data quality and availability, and training and communication within and across organizational boundaries. Continued attention to these organizational, inter-organizational, and implementation dimensions appears as important to the integration of incident reviews in strategic problem-solving initiatives as is the substantive understanding of gun crime that emerges from the reviews themselves.

Notes

1. Braga and Weisburd (2006) offer the interesting observation that even with limited analysis there is evidence of problem-solving efforts having a positive effect on crime and public safety.
2. As of 2013, Detroit and Milwaukee were NIBRS jurisdictions. Indianapolis and St. Louis were not. (Federal Bureau of Investigation 2015a).

Disclosure statement

No potential conflict of interest was reported by the authors.

Funding

This project was supported by Award No. 2013-R2-CX-0015, awarded by the National Institute of Justice, Office of Justice Programs, U.S. Department of Justice. The opinions, findings, and conclusions or recommendations expressed in this publication are those of the author(s) and do not necessarily reflect those of the Department of Justice.

References

Allen, Rhonda Y. W. 2002. "Assessing the Impediments to Organizationasl Change: A View of Community Policing." *Journal of Criminal Justice* 30 (6): 511–517. doi:10.1016/S0047-2352(02)00173-3.

Azrael, Deborah, Anthony A. Braga, and Mallory E. O'Brien. 2013. *Developing the Capacity to Understand and Prevent Homicide: An Evaluation of the Milwaukee Homicide Review Commission*. Boston: Harvard School of Public Health.

Bales, William D., Samuel J. A. Scaggs, Catie L. Clark, David Ensley, and Philip Coltharp. 2014. "Researcher–Practitioner Partnerships: A Case of the Development of a Long-Term Collaborative Project between a University and a Criminal Justice Agency." *Criminal Justice Studies* 27 (3): 294–307. doi:10.1080/1478601X.2014.947807.

Braga, Anthony A. 2008. *Problem-Oriented Policing and Crime Prevention*. 2nd ed. Monsey, NY: Criminal Justice Press.

Braga, Anthony A., and Marianne Hinkle. 2010. "The Participation of Academics in the Criminal Justice Working Group Process." In *The New Criminal Justice: American Communities and the Changing World of Crime Control*, edited by John M. Klofas, Natalie Kroovand Hipple and Edmund F. McGarrell, 114–120. New York: Routeledge.

Braga, Anthony A., David M. Kennedy, Elin J. Waring, and Anne M. Piehl. 2001. "Problem-Oriented Policing, Deterrence, and Youth Violence: An Evaluation of Boston's Operation Ceasefire." *Journal of Research in Crime and Delinquency* 38 (3): 195–225. doi:10.1177/0022427801038003001.

Braga, Anthony A., and David L. Weisburd. 2006. "Problem-Oriented Policing: The Disconnect between Principles and Practice." In *Police Innovation: Contrasting Perspectives*, edited by David L. Weisburd and Anthony A. Braga, 133–154. New York: Cambridge University Press.

Braga, Anthony A., and David L. Weisburd. 2010. *Policing Problem Places: Crime Hot Spots and Effective Prevention*. New York: Oxford University Press.

Braga, Anthony A., David L. Weisburd, Elin J. Waring, Lorraine Green Mazerolle, William Spelman, and Francis Gajewski. 1999. "Problem-Oriented Policing in Violent Crime Places: A Randomized Controlled Experiment." *Criminology* 37 (3): 541–580. doi:10.1111/j.1745-9125.1999.tb00496.x.

Capowich, George E., and Janice A. Roehl. 1994. "Problem-Oriented Policing: Actions and Effectiveness in San Diego." In *The Challenge of Community Policing: Testing the Promises*, edited by Dennis Rosenbaum, 127–146. Thousand Oaks, CA: Sage.

Cordner, Gary W., and Elizabeth Perkins Biebel. 2005. "Problem-Oriented Policing in Practice." *Criminology & Public Policy* 4 (2): 155–180. doi:10.1111/j.1745-9133.2005.00013.x.

Creswell, John W. 2012. *Qualitative Inquiry and Research Design: Choosing among Five Approaches*. Thousand Oaks, CA: Sage publications.

Duffee, David. 1980. *Explaining Criminal Justice: Community Theory and Criminal Justice Reform*. Cambridge, MA: Oelgeschlager, Gunn and Hain Publishers Inc.

Eck, John E., and William Spelman. 1987. *Problem-Solving: Problem-Oriented Policing in Newport News*. Washington, DC: US Department of Justice, National Institute of Justice.

Federal Bureau of Investigation 2015a. "2013 National Incident-Based Reporting System." *U.S. Department of Justice*. Accessed November 30, 2015. https://www.fbi.gov/about-us/cjis/ucr/nibrs/2013/data-tables/#Agency_Tables_by_State

Federal Bureau of Investigation 2015b. *Crime in the United States, 2014*. Washington, DC: United States Department of Justice.

Feeley, Malcolm M. 1983. *Court Reform on Trial: Why Simple Solutions Fail*. New York: Basic Books Inc.

Goldstein, Herman. 1979. "Improving Policing: A Problem-Oriented Approach." *Crime & Delinquency* 25 (2): 236. doi:10.1177/001112877902500207.

Goldstein, Herman. 1990. *Problem-Oriented Policing*. New York: McGraw-Hill Inc.

Greene, Jack R. 2004. "Community Policing and Organization Change." In *Community Policing (Can It Work)?*, edited by Wesley G. Skogan, 30–53. Belmont, CA: Wadsworth.

Grieco, Julie, Heather Vovak, and Cynthia Lum. 2014. "Examining Research-Practice Partnerships in Policing Evaluations." *Policing* 8 (4): 368–378. doi:10.1093/police/pau03.

Hasenfeld, Yeheskel. 1972. "People Processing Organizations: An Exchange Approach." *American Sociological Review* 37 (3): 256–263.

Hasenfeld, Yeheskel, and Paul P. L. Cheung. 1985. "The Juvenile Court as a People-Processing Organization: A Political Economy Perspective." *American Journal of Sociology* 90 (4): 801–824.

Hawken, Angela, and Mark Kleiman. 2009. *Managing Drug Involved Probationers with Swift and Certain Sanctions: Evaluating Hawaii's HOPE*. Washington, DC: U.S. Department of Justice, National Institute of Justice.

Henry, Kelli, and Dana Kralstein. 2011. *Community Courts: The Research Literature*. New York: Center for Court Innovation.

Hutchins, Ellen, Holly Grason, and Arden Handler. 2004. "FIMR and Other Mortality Reviews as Public Health Tools for Strengthening Maternal and Child Health Systems in Communities: Where Do We Need to Go Next?" *Maternal and Child Health Journal* 8 (4): 259–268. doi:10.1023/B:MACI.0000047424.62781.0d.

Klofas, John M., Natalie Kroovand Hipple, Jack McDevitt, Timothy S. Bynum, Edmund F. McGarrell, and Scott H. Decker. 2006. *Project Safe Neighborhoods: Strategic interventions crime incident reviews: Case Study 3, Project Safe Neighborhoods: Strategic Interventions*. Washington, DC: U.S. Department of Justice, Office of Justice Programs.

Klofas, John M., Natalie Kroovand Hipple, and Edmund F. McGarrell. 2010. *The new criminal justice: American communities and the changing world of crime control*. New York: Routledge.

Loftin, Colin. 1986. "Assaultive Violence as a Contagious Social Process." *Bulletin of the New York Academy of Medicine* 62 (5): 550–555.

Loftin, Colin, David McDowall, Karise Curtis, and Matthew D. Fetzer. 2015. "The Accuracy of Supplementary Homicide Report Rates for Large U.S. Cities." *Homicide Studies* 19 (1): 6–27. doi:10.1177/1088767914551984.

Maxfield, Michael G. 1989. "Circumstances in Supplementary Homicide Reports: Variety and Validity." *Criminology* 27 (4): 671–696. doi:10.1111/j.1745-9125.1989.tb01050.x.

McGarrell, Edmund F., Steven Chermak, Jeremy Wilson, and Nicholas Corsaro. 2006. "Reducing Homicide through a "Lever-Pulling" Strategy." *Justice Quarterly* 23 (2): 214–231. doi:10.1080/07418820600688818.

McGarrell, Edmund F., Nicholas Corsaro, Natalie Kroovand Hipple, and Timothy S. Bynum. 2010. "Project Safe Neighborhoods and Violent Crime Trends in US Cities: Assessing Violent Crime Impact." *Journal of Quantitative Criminology* 26 (2): 165–190. doi:10.1007/s10940-010-9091-9.

McGarrell, Edmund F., and Natalie Kroovand Hipple. 2014. "Developing Evidence-Based Crime Prevention Practice: The Dimensions of Effective Implementation." *The Journal of Criminal Investigation and Criminology* 65 (4): 249–258.

Miller, Alden D., Lloyd E. Ohlin, and Robert B. Coates. 1977. *A Theory of Social Reform: Correctional Change Processes in Two States*. Cambridge, MA: Ballinger Publishing Company.

Mitchell, Ojmarrh, David B. Wilson, Amy Eggers, and Doris L. MacKenzie. 2012a. "Assessing the Effectiveness of Drug Courts on Recidivism: A Meta-Analytic Review of Traditional and Non-Traditional Drug Courts." *Journal of Criminal Justice* 40 (1): 60–71. doi:10.1016/j.jcrimjus.2011.11.009.

Mitchell, Ojmarrh, David B. Wilson, Amy Eggers, and Doris L. MacKenzie. 2012b. "Drug Courts' Effects on Criminal Offending for Juveniles and Adults." *Campbell Systematic Reviews* 8 (4). doi:10.4073/csr.2012.4.

O'Brien, Mallory, Laurie Woods, and Ron A. Cisler. 2007. "The Milwaukee Homicide Review Commission: An Interagency Collaborative Process to Reduce Homicide." *Wisconsin Medical Journal* 106 (7): 385–388.

Riedel, Marc. 1990. "Nationwide Homicide Datasets: An Evaluation of UCR and NCHS Data." In *Measuring Crime: Large-Scale, Long-Range Efforts*, edited by Doris L. MacKenzie, Pyyllis J. Baunach and Roy R. Roberg, 175–208. Albany, NY: State Unviersity of New York Press.

Roehl, Janice A., Dennis P. Rosenbaum, Sandra K. Costello, J. Coldren, A. Schuck, Laura Kunard, and D. Forde. 2008. *Paving the Way for Project Safe Neighborhoods: SACSI in 10 US Cities*. Washington, DC: US Department of Justice, Office of Justice Programs, National Institute of Justice.

Rojek, Jeff, Peter Martin, and Geoffrey P. Alpert 2015. "Research Partnerships as a Form of Knowledge Translation." In *Developing and Maintaining Police-Researcher Partnerships to Facilitate Research Use*, 1–25. New York: Springer.

Rojek, Jeff, P. Hayden Smith, and P. Geoffrey Alpert. 2012. "The Prevalence and Characteristics of Police Practitioner-Researcher Partnerships." *Police Quarterly*:241–261. doi: 10.1177/1098611112440698.

Rosenbaum, Dennis P. 1986. *Community Crime Prevention: Does It Work?*. Beverly Hills, CA: Sage Publications.

Sevigny, Eric L., Brian K. Fuleihan, and Frank V. Ferdik. 2013. "Do Drug Courts Reduce the Use of Incarceration?: A Meta-Analysis." *Journal of Criminal Justice* 41 (6): 416–425. doi:10.1016/j.jcrimjus.2013.06.005.

Skogan, Wesley G., and Susan M. Hartnett. 1997. *Community Policing, Chicago Style*. New York: Oxford University Press.

Skogan, Wesley G., Susan M. Hartnett, Jill DuBois, Jennifer T. Comey, Marianne Kaiser, and Justine H. Lovig. 1999. *On the Beat: Police and Community Problem Solving*. Boulder: Westview Press.

Tilley, Nick. 1999. "The Relationship between Crime Prevention and Problem-Oriented Policing." In *Problem-Oriented Policing: Crime-Specific Problems, Critical Issues and Making POP Work*, edited by C. S. Brito and T. Allan, 253–280. Washington, DC: Police Executive Research Forum.

Toch, Hans, and J. Douglas Grant. 1991. *Police as Problem Solvers*. New York: Penum Press.

Wellford, Charles F., John V. Pepper, and Carol V. Petrie, eds. 2005. *Firearms and violence: A critical review. Committee to Improve Research Information and Data on Firearms*. Washington, DC: The National Academies Press.

Williams, Kirk R., and Robert L. Flewelling. 1987. "Family, Acquaintance, and Stranger Homicide: Alternative Procedures for Rate Calculations." *Criminology* 25 (3): 543–560. doi:10.1111/j.1745-9125.1987.tb00810.x.

Wilson, Jeremy M., John M. MacDonald, and George E. Tita. 2010. "Localized Homicide Patterns and Prevention Strategies: A Comparison of Five Project Safe Neighborhood Sites." *Victims & Offenders* 5 (1): 45–63. doi:10.1080/15564880903423060.

Wright, Kevin N. 1981. "The Desirability of Goal Conflict within the Criminal Justice System." *Journal of Criminal Justice* 9 (3): 209–218. doi:10.1016/0047-2352(81)90070-2.

The impact of law enforcement officer perceptions of organizational justice on their attitudes regarding body-worn cameras

Michael J. Kyle and David R. White

ABSTRACT

Civil unrest following recent questionable officer involved shootings and other use of force incidents has prompted public demands for police officers to be equipped with body-worn video cameras (BWCs). As a result of these demands, agencies across the US are rapidly acquiring the devices. While BWCs are widely assumed to be effective tools to document police/citizen encounters, increase law enforcement transparency, and improve both officer and citizen behavior, relatively little research has been conducted in regard to their actual impact. While some preliminary studies have examined officer attitudes concerning the devices, specific factors that potentially affect officer attitudes concerning BWCs and ultimately their level of 'buy-in' have not been examined. The concept of organizational justice is likely one such factor. Through the administration of a survey to a sample of 201 law enforcement officers from four Midwestern and Southern region agencies and those in attendance at regional continuing education venues, the relationship between organizational justice and officer attitudes regarding BWCs is examined. Analysis with structural equation modeling indicates that officer perceptions of organizational justice are a significant factor in terms of their attitudes regarding BWCs.

Introduction

There is perhaps no greater responsibility and yet, no more awkward role to be played by any social actor than that of the modern police officer. They are expected to make clear and thoughtful decisions within the confines of a complex set of laws, in some of life's murkiest situations, and often amid rapidly evolving, stressful confrontations with law violators and obstinate members of society. Their decisions and actions are judged not only through the judicial system and internal police policies, but also through public opinion. While police encounters rarely result in the use of physical force (Adams et al. 1999; Eith and Durose 2011; Garner, Maxwell, and Heraux 2002; Reiss 1973), such instances bring to the forefront what is arguably the most controversial aspect of their role, and many citizens are rightfully concerned with how and why police use force.

Each incident of police use of force must be judged individually and deemed justified under the circumstances. However, as individual cases of police use of force draw national public attention, such as the shooting death of Michael Brown in Ferguson (MO) and choking death of Eric Garner in Staten Island (NY) in 2014, as well as the shooting death of Walter Scott in North Charleston (SC) and in-custody death of Freddie Grey in Baltimore (MD) in 2015, police administrators have become concerned by the loss of legitimacy (Police Executive Research Forum 2015). Indeed, the growth of academic literature concerning procedural justice over the past 25 years demonstrates the importance of the police–citizen contact on citizens' opinions (Bradford 2014; Gau 2014; Tyler and Jackson 2014; Tyler and Sunshine 2003). Consequently, as citizens attempt to evaluate the legitimacy of specific police use of force incidents, the question of video evidence has increasingly been considered as a critical factor. Furthermore, the proliferation of video recorders among the general public – now available on most cellular phones – has increased the likelihood that police–citizen encounters will be recorded. The ability to quickly upload these videos to social media websites, where they risk 'going viral,' or stream (broadcast live) video, increases the likelihood that negative encounters will draw increased attention and discredit to the police agency, and policing more generally.

From an organizational perspective, police administrators are acting quickly to implement body-worn cameras (BWCs) as a way of limiting their liability and ensuring that an official record of police–citizen encounters exists (Roy 2014). However, like the introduction of other technologies or programs, BWCs are not without organizational consequences. They serve to increase the level of surveillance on line-level officers. This raises questions concerning how the videos will be used to critique the officer's conduct, through both internal and external reviews, and therefore, may impact the officers' perceptions of justice within the organizational setting. Organizational justice is defined as one's perception of how fairly they are treated by an organization, and consists of three dimensions: distributive, procedural, and interactional justice (Greenberg and Colquitt 2005).

The current study examines the results of a survey that was designed to test the link between officer perceptions of organizational justice and their opinions concerning the adoption of BWCs. The survey was administered in the spring of 2015 to a sample of just over 200 officers from a variety of small and medium-sized agencies. The results add to a very limited, but growing body of research related to officers' opinions of BWCs, and it furthers the understanding of organizational justice, which has been well established within the organizational theory literature, but sparsely applied by criminal justice scholars.

Background

In a classic Weberian context, the law – as a central part of the rational-legal order – must be endowed with a certain coercive authority (Trubek 1972). And in many ways, police represent the coercive authority of the state, exercising the near exclusive right to use force on citizens (Bittner 1990; Kobler 1975). They are 'boundary actors' in that they exercise their authority in boundary-spanning ways between the formal bureaucracy and the social environment (Prottas 1978). Others have contextualized their role in a more abstract, Durkheimian way – viewing police as helping maintain the normative boundaries of society (Jackson and Sunshine 2007), which might help defend law enforcement's broader 'order maintenance' role.

Recognizing the necessity of law enforcement's right (and responsibility) to use force against the citizenry makes them the object of public scrutiny, and their ability to make discretionary decisions has been viewed as problematic (Lipsky 1980; Prottas 1978). Various police behaviors have been subjected to significant scrutiny at various levels of analysis – from individual, community, and organizational levels (Wolfe and Piquero 2011). Moreover, advances in video technologies have played a role in controlling and monitoring police officer behavior by increasing the visibility, and by extension, the level of transparency in the day-to-day interactions, especially in the traffic stop encounters. However, following the recorded beating of Rodney King by Los Angeles police officers in 1991, and the emergence of widespread accusations of racial profiling, as well as increased drug interdiction (i.e., roadside searches) during the 1990s, law enforcement administrators began to realize the value of video beyond the traffic stop application (Baker 2004; Draisin 2011). Furthermore, the popularity of video recorders among the general public – first camcorders, and now a standard feature of most personal electronic devices such as cell phones – increasingly impacts law enforcement by allowing the public to easily capture video footage of police activities. These videos can now be uploaded immediately to social media websites or shared with mass media outlets (Harris 2010; Goldsmith 2010).

This trend has increased the overall visibility of law enforcement practices and exposed what many would consider distasteful practices, as well as instances of officer misconduct (Goldsmith 2010). However, it may be fair to assume that citizen videos often do not capture the precipitating events leading up to the difficult encounter, which would contextualize the incident. That is, it is only after the citizen realizes the nature of the spectacle that they start recording. To avoid these potential biased depictions, law enforcement executives are compelled to equip their officers with video technology to obtain an 'official record' of police–citizen encounters (Roy 2014). In light of these developments, as well as the increased frequency of civil suits against police officers since the 1960s (Archbold and Maguire 2002), video recordings have proved to be a valuable tool for reducing liability and disproving false allegations against officers, as well as increasing officer accountability (Baker 2004; Farrar 2013; Maghan, O'Reilly, and Shon 2002). Moreover, police administrators found that video recordings of critical incidents were valuable to build public trust through increased transparency (Maghan, O'Reilly, and Shon 2002).

The advent of digital video recording equipment made in-car video systems much more functional, and with the continued focus on liability issues, in-car video became common in law enforcement agencies at every level during the last decade (Harris 2010; White 2014). By 2000, 37% of local departments were using in-car cameras (Hickman and Reaves 2003). This number had increased to 61% by 2007 (Reaves 2010). However, the concept of the 'in-car camera' has always had the disadvantage of only capturing what occurs directly in front of the police vehicle. This limitation, mixed with recent advances in technology, has led to the widespread marketing of BWCs to law enforcement agencies.

While BWCs have received considerable attention recently in the US, they were first utilized in the UK as early as 2005 (White 2014). The recent attention in the US can be attributed, in part, to a 2013 Federal District Court decision regarding racial profiling issues with the NYPD's stop, question, and frisk program, which required officers in the highest offending precincts to be equipped with the devices (White 2014). Since the aforementioned high profile cases, particularly the August 2014, shooting of Michael Brown in Ferguson, the level of attention given to BWCs has drastically increased as evidenced by the $75 million committed by the White House to equip officers with the devices (The White House, Office of the Press Secretary 2015). The incident in Ferguson, which was not captured on video, resulted in conflicting reports between the officer and witnesses, and the backlash caused police administrators to consider the benefits of BWC technology. In fact, the Ferguson Police Department equipped its officers with BWCs only weeks after the Michael Brown shooting (Jennings, Fridell, and Lynch 2014; Stanley 2014). However, little research has been done in regard to the successful implementation of these devices, their impact or best practices for their use.

A recent search of the literature revealed twelve studies that have addressed the implementation and impact of BWCs, five in the UK and seven in the US; however, three of the latter stem from the same project in Mesa, AZ, and only four of the twelve have been published in peer-reviewed journals thus far (Lum et al. 2015). The results of several of these studies indicate that BWCs potentially reduce citizen complaints against officers (Ariel, Farrar, and Sutherland 2015; Goodall 2007; Jennings, Lynch, and Fridell 2015; Katz et al. 2015). Other studies indicate that complaints are resolved more rapidly when officers are BWC equipped (Katz et al. 2015; ODS Consulting 2011). The impact of BWCs on use of force incidents is another potential outcome that has been studied and three of the published studies found significant reductions in use of force incidents (Ariel, Farrar, and Sutherland 2015; Jennings, Lynch, and Fridell 2015; Katz et al. 2015). However, Katz and colleagues (2015) found that BWC equipped officers in Phoenix made more arrests, while Ready and Young (2015) found the opposite in Mesa, AZ. Thus the impact on officer activity levels is uncertain, which may also indicate a difference in officer attitudes or level of 'buy-in' in regard to the devices.

Officer attitudes, which are of particular interest in the current study, have received the least attention; however, one study in Orlando, FL (Jennings, Fridell, and Lynch 2014) and two others in the UK

(Ellis, Jenkins, and Smith 2015; Owens, Mann, and Mckenna 2014) found that officer attitudes regarding the devices are generally positive. What is lacking in the research conducted thus far is the testing of a theoretical framework to attempt to explain officer attitudes concerning BWCs. In this regard, one particular area of interest is the organizational factors that may impact implementation. Like other policies or innovative changes, the successful implementation of BWCs will largely depend on officer buy-in. According to Miller and colleagues (2014):

> One of the primary concerns for police executives is the fear that body-worn cameras will erode the trust between officers and the chief and top managers of the department. Some officers may view the cameras as a signal that their supervisors and managers do not trust them, and they worry that supervisors would use the cameras to track and scrutinize their every move (24).

One method of addressing these concerns, which is taken up in the current study, is to evaluate officers' perceptions of organizational justice as a predictor of their willingness to accept the use of BWCs.

Organizational justice

Organizational theorists have concerned themselves with how people view issues of justice or fairness within their organizational settings (Greenberg and Colquitt 2005). Initially, these ideas focused on the concept of distributive justice, but research has since found the concept to be multidimensional and is now thought to include dimensions of procedural justice, as well as interactional (including both interpersonal and informational) justice under the broader concept of organizational justice (Colquitt 2001). The general thesis that underlies the organizational justice construct is that people's perceptions of fairness in their work environment, both in terms of definable decision outcomes (distributive) and through process-related (procedural) contexts, is related to larger organizational outcomes such as job satisfaction, organizational commitment, evaluation of authority, organizational citizenship behavior, and employee performance (Colquitt et al. 2001). Furthermore, factors such as organizational commitment and organizational citizenship behaviors can be contextualized by an employee's willingness to accept the introduction of a new technology and their willingness to comply with work-rules that may be seen as otherwise limiting their discretion.

As stated earlier, the organizational justice literature initially concerned itself with distributive justice. In this part of the conceptualization 'justice is fostered where outcomes are consistent with implicit norms for allocation, such as equity or equality' (Colquitt 2001, 386). For example, the consistency of pay rates among similarly qualified and positioned individuals within the organization would be considered an issue of distributive justice. As the idea of organizational justice developed, it shifted from an *outcome focus*, to a *process-focused* measure, which grew under the banner of procedural justice. This aspect of justice, first conceived of by Thibaut and Walker (1975) as an issue of 'process control' was extended into organizational contexts by Leventhal (1980), and it may be viewed as the employee's ability to have a voice in the decision-making process or influence over the organizational outcome (Colquitt 2001; Colquitt et al. 2001).

Eventually, this two-factor approach to organizational justice, distributive and procedural, was further developed to include interactional justice. First introduced by Bies and Moag (1986), the interactional justice construct examined the 'quality of interpersonal treatment people received when procedures are implemented' (Colquitt et al. 2001, 426). However, it has since been broken down into two separate dimensions – interpersonal and informational – which have been shown to have independent effects (Colquitt 2001). While interpersonal justice involves interactions between employees and supervisors, which includes such distributive considerations as being treated with respect and a subordinate's perception that their supervisor cares about their well-being and professional development, informational justice relates to procedural aspects by means of the explanations given – information necessary to evaluate the structural aspects of the process (Colquitt et al. 2001). Figure 1 depicts the organizational justice model and its dimensions.

It seems a limited number of policing scholars have utilized the organizational justice construct to predict police officer attitudes and behaviors. According to a 2013 systematic review, this rather

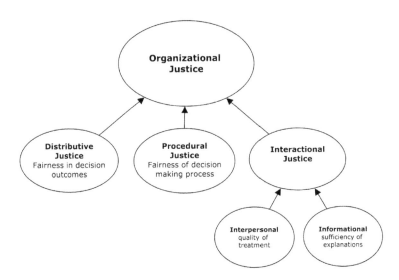

Figure 1. Organizational justice four factor model.

sparse body of literature included five studies that examine organizational justice in a policing context (Roberts and Herrington 2013), and the authors are aware of several others. These studies have examined organizational justice within police agencies and officer well-being (Tinker, Tyler, and Goff 2016; Srivastava 2009); officer willingness to assist citizens, quality of services rendered, and officer willingness to engage in more procedurally just or more democratic forms of policing (Beckley 2014; Myhill and Bradford 2013; Tankebe 2010; Tinker, Tyler, and Goff 2016); officer's job satisfaction, level of organizational commitment, and stress (Crow, Lee, and Joo 2012; Noblet, Rodwell, and Allisey 2009; Tankebe 2010); officer misconduct (Wolfe and Piquero 2011), and officer compliance with policy and procedure (Haas et al. 2015; Tyler, Callahan, and Frost 2007). Others have more generally considered the role of trust and transparency in organizational justice (Schafer 2013), while some have examined the importance of organizational justice on officer's self-legitimacy (i.e., confidence in their own authority), and how self-legitimacy affects officer's willingness to engage in more democratic forms of policing (Bradford and Quinton 2014; Tinker, Tyler, and Goff 2016).

While these scholars have used a variety of conceptual frameworks to measure the elements of organizational justice (i.e., procedural, distributive, interpersonal, and informational), and they have operationalized these measures differently, their findings have consistently confirmed the importance of organizational justice to the various contexts. However, the examination of police officer perceptions of organizational justice and their attitudes regarding any innovation seems to be notably absent from the literature. In the current analysis, it is not difficult to establish the theoretical bridge between officers' attitudes of organizational justice, and their willingness to accept the introduction of BWCs. This is true for several reasons.

First, BWCs represent the introduction of a significant new technology, which in and of itself may be reason to consider the importance of officer buy-in. That is, the degree to which management involves officers in the decision-making process and how much information or control they share, both in the normative and instrumental aspects of the decision, all have a potential connection with how fair or just officers may see their overall work environment. Important issues include, but are not limited to, how well management communicates the need for the change, how involved the officers are in assessing product quality or functionality, how much training is to be offered, and how clearly the timeline of implementation is communicated.

Second, while an organization's internal policies may collectively construct a framework from which employees can make meaningful assessments of fairness (and justice) in both distributive and procedural contexts, policies related to BWCs will have deeper implications, as they will relate to both internal and external complaint investigation procedures. Of all the policies within a police organization, those that are likely to draw the most fire from officers for being either 'just' or 'unjust' are those policies that deal with how they are treated in complaint investigations (De Angelis and Kupchik 2007). In today's world, many agencies are bound by union contracts and even state laws to follow certain procedures in investigating allegations of police misconduct. The institutionalized nature of these broader mandates demonstrates the sense of justice officers want when they are accused of wrong-doing.

Finally, while officers' perceptions of organizational justice may be defined within the organizational setting, the external environment may produce some more global fears over how BWC video of particular incidents may be used against the officer in civil or criminal proceedings. The popular media coverage of the implementation and use of BWCs stemming from the aforementioned high profile cases may make officers more conscious of how their particular agency considers and implements the devices. Thus, it seems highly likely that in order to achieve officer buy-in and ensure successful implementation, issues of organizational justice will be important.

Method

In order to explore what, if any, impact that perceptions of organizational justice might have on officer attitudes regarding BWCs, and whether any such relationship might vary by an officer's capacity/assignment, rank, experience with BWCs, disciplinary history, individual demographic characteristics, and/or their employing agency type and size, the investigators sought to survey a diverse sample of officers. Data for the current study were collected from a convenience sample of 201 officers in two adjoining states (one in the Midwest & one in the South). Surveys were administered in the spring of 2015 during roll calls at one small (<24 full-time sworn) and three medium-sized municipal police departments (78, 78, and 103 authorized, full-time sworn personnel). Other full-time sworn officers that were on duty at the time of these roll calls were also encouraged to participate in the survey since it was recognized that the introduction of BWCs is not strictly a patrol-related issue.

In addition to the surveys administered at individual departments, permission was obtained from one state's law enforcement standards and training authority to administer the survey in two 40-hour continuing education training courses. The continuing education courses, which accounted for 55 participants, were open to all ranks of sworn law enforcement officers, but were attended primarily by patrol officers and detectives. These continuing education venues consisted of a basic domestic violence investigation course (26 in attendance) and a crime scene management course (30 in attendance), which provided the sample with officers from municipal police (22) and sheriff's departments (28), as well as one state police agency (5). Of these 55 participants, 31 were employed at an agency of 24 or fewer sworn, 13 were from agencies of 25 to 49 sworn, 6 from agencies of 50 to 99, and 5 were employed by agencies of 100 or more sworn officers. Participation was voluntary and 201 of the 204 officers eligible completed the survey for a response rate of 98.5%.

The descriptive statistics of the sample ($n = 201$) are presented in Table 1. The sample was 81% male, 79% white, and the average age of the participants was 38. In terms of education level, 9.5% were high school graduates with no college, 35% had some college, but no degree, 17.5% had an Associate's degree, 32% had Bachelor's degrees, and 6% had a Master's degree or higher. The mean years of service was 12.9; 76.9% were assigned to patrol as their primary function, and 51% were at the rank of patrol officer, 29.3% were detectives, 16.2% held the rank of Sergeant or higher, and 3.5% held what they considered another ranked position that was not specified. The majority of participants (83.5%) were employed by police departments, 14% were employed by sheriff's departments and 2.50% by state police agencies. Lastly, 20% of the sample was employed by agencies of 24 sworn officers or less, 8% by those with 25–49, 56.5% with 50–99, and 15.5% with 100 + sworn officers.

Table 1. Descriptive statistics – officer demographics ($n = 201$).

Officer demographics	M/%
Officer gender	
Male	81.80
Female	18.20
Officer race	
White	79.50
Black	16.00
Other	4.50
Officer age	38.61*
Officer years of experience	12.92**
Officer education level	
High school	9.50
Some college-no degree	35.00
Associate's degree	17.50
Bachelor's degree	32.00
Master's degree or higher	6.00
Department type	
Municipal police department	83.10
Sheriff's department	13.90
State police	2.50
Other	0.50
Officer's department size	
24 or less	20.00
25 to 49	8.00
50 to 99	56.50
100 or more	15.50
Officer capacity	
Patrol	76.90
Investigations	12.60
Admin/Support	4.50
Other	6.00
Officer rank	
Patrol officer	51.00
Detective	29.30
Sergeant	7.60
Lieutenant	5.10
Captain or higher	3.50
Other	3.50
Officer's agency implemented BWCs	26.40

*SD 9.34 Minimum 22.00/Maximum 65.00; **SD 8.89 Minimum 0.00/Maximum 43.00.

Measures

Dependent variable

The dependent variable, attitudes regarding BWCs, was measured with six survey items, which were summed to create an index score ranging from 0 to 30. The BWC attitudinal items were based on questions used by Jennings and colleagues (2014) in their assessment of the attitudes of Orlando police officers concerning BWCs. The BWC survey items included four questions that addressed protection of the officer and the agency, and two questions that addressed citizen behavior. The protection items included the following questions: (1) *I would feel safer using a body-worn camera*; (2) *Equipping officers with body-worn cameras would protect both the officer and the agency*; (3) *I would feel comfortable using a body-worn camera*; and (4) *I believe that my agency should equip all officers with body-worn cameras*. The citizen behavior questions included: (1) *The use of body-worn cameras would increase citizen compliance with officer directives*; and (2) *Equipping officers with body-worn cameras would reduce citizen complaints against officers*. A 5-point Likert scale was utilized for responses to these six survey items, which consisted of: *1 = Strongly Disagree; 2 = Disagree; 3 = Neither Agree nor Disagree; 4 = Agree; 5 = Strongly Agree*.

Independent variables

Organizational justice is a latent construct that, as discussed earlier, is thought to consist of four dimensions: distributive justice, procedural justice, interpersonal justice, and informational justice. Three of these four dimensions were measured utilizing survey items adapted from Wolfe and Piquero (2011) and Colquitt (2001). Of these survey items, four measured procedural justice and included: (1) *Disciplinary actions are handled in a fair and consistent manner*; (2) *Promotions and appointments to special assignments depend on who you know, not merit*; (3) *The rules and regulations dealing with officer conduct are fair and sensible*; and (4) *When accused of wrongdoing, officers are provided a fair opportunity to present their version of the events*. Interpersonal justice was measured by two survey items including: (1) *My immediate supervisor(s) treat me with respect and dignity*; and (2) *My immediate supervisor cares about my professional development*. Lastly, informational justice was measured with two survey items, which included: (1) *My supervisors and command staff have been candid in their communications with me*; and (2) *My supervisors and command staff explain policy and procedures thoroughly*.

As with the dependent variable attitudes regarding BWCs, the aforementioned survey items, designed as observable indicators of the latent organizational justice construct, were measured with a 5-point Likert scale consisting of: *1 = Strongly Disagree; 2 = Disagree; 3 = Neither Agree nor Disagree; 4 = Agree; 5 = Strongly Agree*. The second procedural justice indicator, *Promotions and appointments to special assignments depend on who you know, not merit,* was, however, reverse coded as follows: *5 = Strongly Disagree; 4 = Disagree; 3 = Neither Agree nor Disagree; 2 = Agree; 1 = Strongly Agree.*

In addition to these indicators of organizational justice, nine other variables are thought to potentially have an impact on officer attitudes regarding body worn cameras, and thus are controlled for in the analysis. These variables included rank, assignment/capacity, race, gender, level of education, whether the agency where the officer is employed has implemented BWCs, whether the officer had any citizen complaints filed against him or her in the previous 24 months, the officer's department type, and the size of their agency. These control variables were coded as follows: rank was categorized as patrol officer, detective, sergeant, lieutenant, captain or higher, or other, and assignment/capacity was categorized as patrol, investigations, administration/support, or other. Race was coded 0 = nonwhite and 1 = white and gender was coded 1 = male and 2 = female. Level of education was categorized as high school/GED, some college/no degree, associate's degree, bachelor's degree, or masters/professional degree. The two binary variables, whether the officer's agency had implemented BWCs and whether the officer had any citizen complaints filed against them in the previous 24 months, were coded as 0 = no and 1 = yes. Department type was categorized as municipal police department, sheriff's department, or other, and agency size was categorized in ranges of 24 or less, 25–49, 50–99, and 100 or more.

Data analysis

The analysis consisted of structural equation modeling utilizing Mplus Version 5.1 statistical software's weighted least squares mean and variance adjusted estimator (WLSMV), which is appropriate for the estimation of models with categorical indicator variables (Muthén and Muthén 2008). First, the proposed model was evaluated with the Mplus goodness-of-fit indices, which include chi-square and the associated p-value, the CFI (comparative fit index), TLI (Tucker-Lewis index), and RMSEA (root mean square error of approximation). The guidelines for interpreting these indices (Byrne 2012; Gau 2010) are as follows. The chi-square test ideally should not be significant ($p < .05$). To have a significant result of the chi-square test may indicate a poor fitting model as Gau (2010) points out, 'a significant chi-square value means there is a significant difference between the theorized and the observed covariance matrices' (144). However, while a significant finding in the chi-square result may indicate that the model is problematic, it generally should be viewed with some caution as sample size may lead to erroneous chi-square results, especially in large samples (Byrne 2012; Gau 2010). According to both Byrne (2012) and Gau (2010) the model should be evaluated in terms of other fit indices as well.

The CFI (comparative fit index) ranges from 0.0 to 1.0 (1.0 is the upper boundary) and values above .90 indicate a good fit. The TLI (Tucker-Lewis index), on the other hand, may exceed 1.0. Therefore, for the TLI, a good fitting model is indicated by a value above .90, but below 1.2 (Byrne 2012; Gau 2010). The RMSEA (root mean square error of approximation) is based on a value of 0. The closer to 0 the RMSEA is the better the fit of the model. Generally, RMSEAs less than .06 indicate a very good fit, .06 to .10 indicate a reasonable fit, and above .10 indicate a poorly fitting model (Byrne 2012; Gau 2010).

Results

The means and standard deviations, as well as the Pearson correlations are reported for the observed variables in Table 2. Aside from the expected correlations observed between the observed individual measures of the latent constructs of *organizational justice* and *BWC Attitudes*, no multicollinearity issues were detected ($r < 0.70$ and variance inflation factors for all independent variables <3.00).

As described above, the measurement of the observed indicators of organizational justice was divided between three dimensions (procedural, interpersonal, and informational). The descriptive statistics of these observed indicators are presented in Table 3 below. These observed indicators are represented by *Procedural 1, 2, 3 & 4; Interpersonal 1 & 2;* and *Informational 1 & 2* in the organizational justice structural equation model. Before presenting the full model, the aforementioned measurement model of organizational justice is presented in Figure 2. Although the structural model for organizational justice had a significant chi-square result ($p = .0192$), the CFI was .989, the TLI was .993, and the RMSEA was 0.071 indicating a reasonable goodness-of-fit. The model depicted in Figure 2 includes the pathway coefficients which also indicate a good fit ($b > 0.400$).

As mentioned, the observed indicators of officer attitudes regarding BWCs addressed officer and agency protection and citizen behavior. The descriptive statistics for these observed indicators are provided in Table 4 below. The full model follows in Figure 3. The goodness-of-fit indices for the full model are as follows. The chi-square test result was 39.677 ($p = 0.0894$), the CFI was .990, the TLI was .988, and the RMSEA was 0.044, all indicating a good fitting model.

Testing of the model indicated that officer perceptions of organizational justice had a significant impact on their attitudes regarding BWCs ($b = 0.868, p = 0.001$). In addition, three of the other independent variables were significant predictors of BWC attitudes. First, whether or not the officer's agency had implemented BWCs was significant ($b = 1.434, p = 0.034$), with officers whose agencies had implemented the devices holding more positive attitudes regarding them. Second, rank emerged as a significant predictor ($b = 1.083, p = 0.002$), demonstrating a positive relationship between rank and BWC attitudes. Gender was also a significant predictor of attitudes regarding BWCs ($b = 1.456, p = 0.032$), with females holding more positive attitudes regarding BWCs than males. However, none of the other variables (an officer's assignment/ capacity, his or her race, education level, size and type of the agency where they are employed, nor whether or not they had a citizen complaint filed against them) emerged as significant predictors of an officer's attitudes regarding BWCs. The r^2 value of 0.189 indicates the model explains about 19% of the variance in officer attitudes regarding BWCs. The structural model coefficients are reported in Table 5 below.

Discussion

While the recent attention toward BWCs will unquestionably spur a significant amount of research, many of the efforts (we believe) will likely be directed at whether or not BWCs change behaviors of both police officers and citizens. Unfortunately, such efforts will do little to advance our theoretical understanding of police conduct. Conversely, organizational justice appears to be a viable theoretical construct from which we may better understand some of the normative aspects underlying police behavior. As it relates here, the results indicated that officers' perceptions of organizational justice were a significant predictor of their opinions toward BWCs. The additional finding that experience with BWCs is a significant predictor of more positive attitudes toward the devices is also important.

Table 2. Correlations, means, and standard deviations for observed variables.

Variable	1	2	3	4	5	6	7	8	9	10	11	12	13	14	15	16	17	18	19	20	21	22	23	24
(1) Q1a	1.055																							
(2) Q1b	.347**	1.131																						
(3) Q1c	.660**	.282**	.886																					
(4) Q1d	.495**	.233**	.591**	.866																				
(5) Q1e	.339**	.161*	.371**	.422**	.730																			
(6) Q1f	.412**	.265**	.478**	.456**	.693**	.919																		
(7) Q1g	.513**	.347**	.468**	.537**	.433**	.526**	1.058																	
(8) Q1h	.542**	.263**	.545**	.509**	.423**	.538**	.623**	1.058																
(9) Q2a	.072	.055	.183**	.214**	.133	.140*	.230**	.067	.942															
(10) Q2b	.072	.045	.190**	.242**	.135	.116	.218**	.101	.692**	.899														
(11) Q2c	.067	.059	.150*	.216**	.189**	.127	.159*	.073	.608**	.724**	.907													
(12) Q2d	.092	.121	.160*	.199**	.126	.159*	.245**	.096	.756**	.712**	.700**	1.072												
(13) Q2i	-.003	.045	.047	.170*	.002	.043	.249**	.111	.372**	.341**	.256**	.375**	1.082											
(14) Q2j	.067	.044	.146*	.158*	.040	.106	.212**	.161*	.360**	.359**	.232**	.287**	.711**	1.136										
(15) Rank	.074	.123	.144*	.001	.018	.068	.105	-.011	.233**	.234**	.123	.255**	.085	.046	.782									
(16) Race	-.130	-.169*	-.094	-.117	-.123	-.032	-.165*	-.156*	-.016	-.066	-.101	-.102	-.034	.037	-.091	.405								
(17) Gender	-.021	.074	-.039	.014	-.101	-.031	.073	.061	.187**	.210**	.089	.165*	.067	.154*	.057	-.062	.387							
(18) Education	.011	-.013	.001	.036	.125	.069	.070	-.025	.058	.110	.044	.066	.071	.000	.136	-.198**	.129	.442						
(19) Agency 3WCs	.020	.015	-.038	-.071	.067	.076	.177*	.072	.172*	.142*	.129	.258**	.156*	.091	.166*	-.088	.119	.123	.469					
(20) Capacity	.079	.124	.136	.029	-.025	-.001	.185**	.085	.079	.048	-.004	.040	.070	.094	.377**	-.026	.040	.005	.087	.834				
(21) Dept. Size	-.128	-.080	-.093	-.068	.103	.072	-.114	-.053	-.117	-.120	-.097	-.140*	-.013	-.144*	-.127	.124	.013	.220**	.003	-.222**	.966			
(22) Dept. Type	-.009	-.005	-.010	.138	.151*	.157*	-.008	.053	-.038	-.053	-.003	-.136	-.059	-.113	-.036	.072	.036	.214**	-.259**	-.121	.486**	.391		
(23) Complaints	-.086	-.070	.031	.148*	-.022	-.082	-.038	-.035	.031	-.033	.042	-.037	-.087	-.122	-.163*	-.029	-.032	-.027	-.084	-.108	.114	.077	1.134	
(24) BWC Atts	.086	.080	.191**	.244**	.162*	.155*	.241*	.095	.869**	.883**	.856**	.909**	.385**	.349**	.241**	-.078	.186**	.078	.205**	.048	-.132	-.065	.001	4.588
Minimum	1	1	1	1	1	1	1	1	1	1	1	1	1	1	1	0	0	1	0	1	1	1	0	6
Maximum	5	5	5	5	5	5	5	5	5	5	5	5	5	5	6	1	1	5	1	4	4	3	1	30
Mean	3.46	2.99	3.72	3.80	4.33	4.01	3.54	3.46	2.92	3.62	3.60	3.20	2.47	2.60	.69	.80	1.18	.26	.32	1.40	2.68	1.89	13.33	18.39

Notes: Standard deviation reported in the correlation matrix diagonal.
*$p < 0.05$; **$p < 0.01$.

Table 3. Descriptive statistics for observed indicators (Independent variables) – Organizational justice.

Indicator	M	SD	FL
Procedural Justice			.888
Q1a: Disciplinary actions are handled in a fair and consistent manner.	3.45	1.055	.819
Q1b: Promotions and appointments to special assignments depend on who you know, not merit.	3.01	1.131	.443
Q1c: The rules and regulations dealing with officer conduct are fair and sensible.	3.72	.886	.878
Q1d: When accused of wrongdoing, officers are provided a fair opportunity to present their version of the events.	3.80	.866	.815
Interpersonal Justice			.766
Q1e: My immediate supervisor(s) treat me with respect and dignity.	4.33	.730	.835
Q1f: My immediate supervisor cares about my professional development.	4.01	.919	.954
Informational Justice			.994
Q1 g: My supervisors and command staff have been candid in their communications with me.	3.54	1.058	.822
Q1 h: My supervisors and command staff explain policy and procedures thoroughly.	3.46	1.058	.842

Notes: Likert scale: (All items except *Pro 2) 1 = Strongly Disagree; 2 = Disagree; 3 = Neither Agree nor Disagree; 4 = Agree; 5 = Strongly Agree.
(*Pro 2 reverse coded).
All items – Minimum = 0/Maximum = 5.

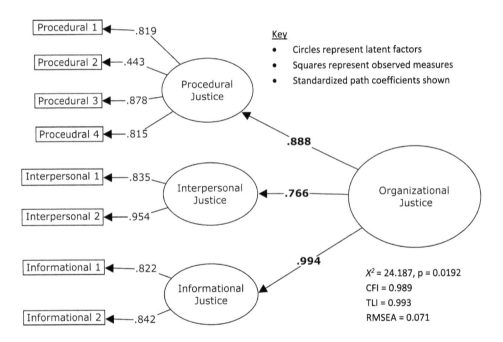

Figure 2. Structural model for organizational justice.

This may come as no surprise, since like any change effort; some of the initial fears over change may be lost after implementation. Additionally, the fact that female and higher ranking officers tend to have more positive attitudes concerning BWCs should be explored in more detail. There are good theoretical reasons to believe that these two groups may see some of these issues through different lenses. These findings collectively demonstrate that agencies considering implementing BWCs should first consider issues of organizational justice within their agency.

However, the study is not without some limitations. First, the model lacked indicators for the dimension of distributive justice. While perhaps less significant here than in other organizational contexts, policing scholars should attempt to identify better measures of the distributive contexts of organizational justice. Second, two of the dimensions, interpersonal and Informational justice had only two

Table 4. Descriptive statistics for observed indicators (Dependent variable) – Attitudes regarding BWCs.

Indicators in BWC attitudes index	*M*	SD
Q2a: I would feel safer using a body-worn camera	2.92	.942
Q2b: Equipping officers with body-worn cameras would protect both the officer and the agency	3.62	.899
Q2c: I would feel comfortable using a body-worn camera	3.60	.907
Q2d: I believe that my agency should equip all officers with body-worn cameras.	3.20	1.072
Q2i: The use of body-worn cameras would increase citizen compliance with officer directives.	2.47	1.082
Q2f: Equipping officers with body-worn cameras would reduce citizen complaints against officers.	2.60	1.136

Notes: Likert scale: 1 = Strongly Disagree; 2 = Disagree; 3 = Neither Agree nor Disagree; 4 = Agree; 5 = Strongly Agree.
All items – Minimum = 0/Maximum = 5.

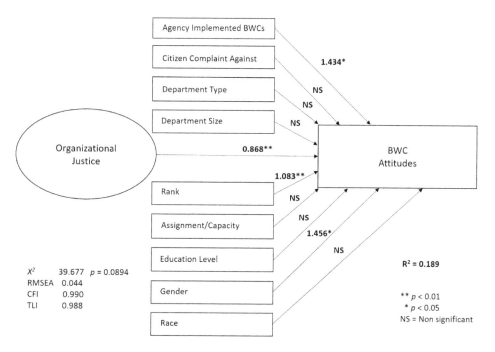

Figure 3. Structural model for officer perceptions of organizational justice and attitudes regarding BWCs.

indicators. Increasing those numbers to four each, as well as adding distributive justice indicators could potentially make the model more robust. Third, behavioral indicators need to be developed, as it seems likely that this is an important dimension of officer attitudes regarding BWCs. As it stands, we have measured officer attitudes regarding BWCs as a unidimensional concept through summing the values of the six indicator items we utilized into an index score. However, we suspect that officer attitudes regarding BWCs may in fact be a multidimensional concept. A more robust and comprehensive set of indicators needs to be developed to include items to gauge whether officers believe they have, or would alter how they perform their duties or the quantity of self-initiated activities as a result of being equipped with a BWC. With a more robust set of indicators across a few dimensions of the concept a second-order model such as the model we developed for organizational justice might be possible.

Lastly, the sample was comprised of mostly small and medium-sized agencies located in a relatively small geographic region. However, a review of the 2013 LEMAS data (the most recent available) revealed that across that sample the mean proportion of patrol officers was 56%, the mean proportion of investigative personnel was 14%, the mean proportion of other support roles was 12%, and 18% were in a supervisory or executive role. While detectives were somewhat oversampled in the current study, the overall numbers seem reasonably representative of the averages found in the latest LEMAS data. Nevertheless, one must be cautious when interpreting the generalizability of this study. Keeping

Table 5. Structural model coefficients for officer attitudes regarding BWCs.

Indicators	b	SE	p-value
Organizational justice	0.868**	0.269	0.001
Agency implemented BWCs	1.434*	0.677	0.034
Rank	1.083**	0.342	0.002
Assignment/Capacity	−0.433	0.328	0.187
Gender	1.456*	0.679	0.032
Race	0.126	0.636	0.842
Education level	0.155	0.233	0.507
Department/Agency size	−0.570	0.323	0.078
Department/Agency type	0.329	0.892	0.712
Citizen complaint filed against officer	0.415	0.497	0.403

$^*p < 0.05; ^{**}p < 0.01.$

these caveats in mind, this study has established that the indicators utilized for the measurement of three dimensions of organizational justice in the policing context fit well in a structural equation model, and that officer perceptions of organizational justice have a significant impact on their attitudes regarding BWCs.

Implications

In order to achieve a high level of officer buy-in, administrators should consider some of the following ways to improve implementation. First, administrators should not jump haphazardly into the implementation of any new technology, particularly one like BWCs that has direct and indirect implications for internal and external investigations of wrongdoing. From ensuring the devices are functional and practical for everyday use, to increasing the line officers' understanding of the need for change, administrators should attempt to keep employees informed and allow them to have input in the decision-making process.

Second, administrators who successfully convince officers of the need for change, and who involve them in the trial process, should also consider very carefully how they address the needed policy changes. Agency policies represent an important framework by which all employees come to understand the agency's expectations, as well as the procedural methods for addressing issues. In simpler terms, it helps the employees decide what seems just or unjust within their organizational context. Therefore, as employees begin to consider how BWC video will impact them, they will expect that the web of policies related to BWCs seems rational. If policy seems irrational, or seems constructed in such a way as to unfairly skew things toward management, line-level officers are likely to reject the policies and could easily circumvent the authority.

Finally, administrators should consider focusing on the learning aspects of BWCs as a way of helping officers see the more positive aspects potentially associated with new public expectation. That is, for years many training academies have shown recruit officers the in-car videos of incidents in which things went wrong. Traffic stops where officers were killed because of complacency or because they failed to recognize indicators that things were about to turn violent. These videos, by and large, help officers learn from the mistakes of others.

Conclusion

In addition to the organizational justice framework explaining, at least in part, officer attitudes toward BWCs, it seems more important to recognize the potential explanatory power of organizational justice in the broader context of police work. Criminal justice scholars are keenly aware of the concepts of distributive and procedural justice within literature on police legitimacy, but they have done less to apply these ideas to the organizational setting, with a few encouraging exceptions. Specifically, scholars should continue to concentrate on the impact organizational justice has on police officers' attitudes and actions in the field. The fact that officers' perceptions of organizational justice help explain their perceptions of BWCs is not surprising, but it seems (we believe) to be an indicator of something much larger. Officers' willingness to accept organizational change; to accept new technologies, particularly those that serve to increase surveillance over their daily actions; their more general attitudes toward trust and transparency, and their attitudes toward how these things intersect with an increasingly hostile public scrutiny demonstrate that scholars should continue to examine the importance of the organizational justice framework.

Disclosure statement

No potential conflict of interest was reported by the authors.

References

Adams, K., G. P. Alpert, R. G. Dunham, L. A. G. Garner, M. A. Henriquez, P. A. Langan, C. D. Maxwell, and S. K. Smith. 1999. *Use of Force by Police: Overview of National and Local Data Series: Research Report.* Washington, DC: U.S. Department of Justice, Office of Justice Programs.

Archbold, C. A., and E. R. Maguire. 2002. "Studying Civil Suits against the Police: A Serendipitous Finding of Sample Selection Bias." *Police Quarterly* 5 (2): 222–249.

Ariel, B., W. A. Farrar, and A. Sutherland. 2015. "The Effect of Police Body-worn Cameras on Use of Force and Citizens' Complaints against the Police: A Randomized Controlled Trial." *Journal of Quantitative Criminology* 31 (3): 509–535.

Baker, W. G. 2004. *The Impact of Video Evidence on Modern Policing. IACP Report to National Institute of Justice.* Alexandria, VA: International Association of Chiefs of Police.

Beckley, A. 2014. "Organisational Justice: Is the Police Service Ready for It?" *Journal of Policing, Intelligence and Counter Terrorism* 9 (2): 176–190.

Bies, R. J., and J. F. Moag. 1986. "Interactional Justice: Communication Criteria of Fairness." In *Research on Negotiations in Organizations*, Vol. 1, edited by R. J. Lewicki, B. H. Sheppard, and M. H. Bazerman, 43–55. Greenwich, CT: JAI Press.

Bittner, E. 1990. "Florence Nightingale in Pursuit of Willie Sutton." In *Aspects of Police Work*, edited by E. Bittner, 233–268. Boston, MA: Northeastern University Press.

Bradford, B. 2014. "Policing and Social Identity: Procedural Justice, Inclusion and Cooperation between Police and Public." *Policing and Society* 24 (1): 22–43.

Bradford, B., and P. Quinton. 2014. "Self-legitimacy, Police Culture and Support for Democratic Policing in an English Constabulary." *British Journal of Criminology* 54: 1023–1046.

Byrne, B. 2012. *Structural Equation Modeling with Mplus: Basic Concepts, Applications, and Programming.* New York: Routledge.

Colquitt, J. A. 2001. "On the Dimensionality of Organizational Justice: A Construct Validation of a Measure." *Journal of Applied Psychology* 86 (3): 386–400.

Colquitt, J. A., D. E. Conlon, M. J. Wesson, C. Porter, and K. Y. Ng. 2001. "Justice at the Millennium: A Meta-analytic Review of 25 Years of Organizational Justice Research." *Journal of Applied Psychology* 86 (3): 425–445.

Crow, M. S., C. B. Lee, and J. J. Joo. 2012. "Organisational Justice and Organizational Commitment among South Korean Police Officers: An Investigation of Job Satisfaction as a Mediator." *Policing: An International Journal of Police Strategies & Management* 35 (2): 402–423.

De Angelis, J., and A. Kupchik. 2007. "Citizen Oversight, Procedural Justice, and Officer Perceptions of the Complaint Investigation Process." *Policing: An International Journal of Police Strategies & Management* 30 (4): 651–671.

Draisin, L. 2011. *Police Technology: An Analysis of In-car Cameras and Body Worn Cameras*. Orlando: University of Central Florida.

Eith, C., and M. R. Durose. 2011. *Contacts between Police and the Public, 2008*. Washington, DC: Bureau of Justice Statistics.

Ellis, T., T. Jenkins, and P. Smith. 2015. *Evaluation of the Introduction of Personal Issue Body Worn Video Cameras (Operation Hyperion) on the Isle of Wright: Final Report to Hampshire Constabulary*. Portsmouth: University of Portsmouth, Institute of Criminal Justice Studies.

Farrar, W. 2013. *Self-awareness to Being Watched and Socially-desirable Behavior: A Field Experiment on the Effect of Body-worn Cameras and Police Use-of-force*. Washington, DC: Police Foundation.

Garner, J. H., C. D. Maxwell, and C. G. Heraux. 2002. "Characteristics Associated with the Prevalence and Severity of Force Used by the Police." *Justice Quarterly* 19 (4): 705–746.

Gau, J. M. 2010. "Basic Principles and Practices of Structural Equation Modeling in Criminal Justice and Criminology Research." *Journal of Criminal Justice Education* 21 (2): 136–151.

Gau, J. M. 2014. "Procedural Justice and Police Legitimacy: A Test of Measurement and Structure." *American Journal of Criminal Justice* 39 (2): 187–205.

Goldsmith, A. J. 2010. "Policing's New Visibility." *British Journal of Criminology* 50 (5): 914–934.

Goodall, M. 2007. *Guidance for the Police Use of Body-worn Video Devices*. London: Home Office.

Greenberg, J., and J. A. Colquitt, eds. 2005. *Handbook of Organizational Justice*. New York: Erlbaum Associates.

Haas, N. E., M. Van Craen, W. G. Skogan, and D. M. Fleitas. 2015. "Explaining Officer Compliance: The Importance of Procedural Justice and Trust inside a Police Organization." *Criminology and Criminal Justice* 15 (4): 442–463.

Harris, D. A. 2010. *Picture This: Body Worn Video Devices ('Head Cams') as Tools for Ensuring Fourth Amendment Compliance by Police*. Legal Studies Research Paper Series. Pittsburgh, PA: University of Pittsburgh School of Law.

Hickman, M. J., and B. A. Reaves. 2003. *Local Police Departments, 2000*. Washington, DC: Department of Justice, Bureau of Justice Statistics.

Jackson, J., and J. Sunshine. 2007. "Public Confidence in Policing: A neo-Durkheimian Perspective." *British Journal of Criminology* 47 (2): 214–233.

Jennings, W. G., L. A. Fridell, and M. D. Lynch. 2014. "Cops and Cameras: Officer Perceptions of the Use of Body-worn Cameras in Law Enforcement." *Journal of Criminal Justice* 42 (6): 549–556.

Jennings, W. G., M. Lynch, and L. A. Fridell. 2015. "Evaluating the Impact of Police Officer Body-worn Cameras (BWCs) on Response-to-resistance and Serious External Complaints: Evidence from the Orlando Police Department (OPD) Experience Utilizing a Randomized Controlled Experiment." *Journal of Criminal Justice* 43 (6): 480–486.

Katz, C. M., M. Kurtenbach, D. W. Choate, and M. D. White. 2015. *Phoenix, Arizona, Smart Policing Initiative: Evaluating the Impact of Police Officer Body-worn Cameras*. Washington, DC: U.S. Department of Justice, Bureau of Justice Assistance.

Kobler, A. L. 1975. "Police Homicide in a Democracy." *Journal of Social Issues* 31 (1): 163–184.

Leventhal, G. S. 1980. "What Should be Done with Equity Theory? New Approaches to the Study of Fairness in Social Relationships." In *Social Exchange: Advances in Theory and Research*, edited by K. Gergen, M. Greenberg, and R. Willis, 27–55. New York: Plenum Press.

Lipsky, D. 1980–2010. *Street-level Bureaucracy: Dilemmas of the Individual in Public Services*. 30th Anniversary ed. New York: Russell Sage Foundation.

Lum, C., C. S. Koper, L. M. Merola, A. Scherer, and A. Reioux. 2015. *Existing and Ongoing Body Worn Camera Research: Knowledge Gaps and Opportunities*. Report for the Laura and John Arnold Foundation. Fairfax, VA: Center for Evidence-Based Crime Policy, George Mason University.

Maghan, J., G. W. O'Reilly, and P. C. H. Shon. 2002. "Technology, Policing, and Implications of In-car Videos." *Police Quarterly* 5 (1): 25–42.

Miller, L., J. Toliver, and Police Executive Research Forum. 2014. *Implementing a Body-Worn Camera Program: Recommendations and Lessons Learned*. Washington, DC: Office of Community Oriented Policing Services.

Muthén, B. O., and L. K. Muthén. 2008. *Mplus*. Los Angeles, CA: Muthén & Muthén.

Myhill, A., and Bradford, B. 2013. "Overcoming Cop Culture? Organisational Justice and Police Officers' Attitudes toward the Public." *Policing: An International Journal of Police Strategies & Management* 36 (2): 338–356.

Noblet, A. J., J. J. Rodwell, and A. F. Allisey. 2009. "Police Stress: The Role of the Psychological Contract and Perceptions of Fairness." *Policing: An International Journal of Police Strategies & Management* 32 (4): 613–630.

ODS Consulting. 2011. *Body Worn Video Projects in Paisley and Aberdeen, Self-evaluation*. Glasgow: ODS Consulting.

Owens, C., D. Mann, and R. Mckenna. 2014. *The Essex BWV Trial: The Impact of BWV on Criminal Justice Outcomes of Domestic Abuse Incidents*. London: College of Policing.

Police Executive Research Forum. 2015. *Critical Issues in Policing Series: Re-engineering Training on Police Use of Force*. Washington, DC: Police Executive Research Forum.

Prottas, J. M. 1978. "The Power of the Street-level Bureaucrat in Public Service Bureaucracies." *Urban Affairs Review* 13 (3): 285–312.

Ready, J. T., and J. T. Young. 2015. "The Impact of On-officer Video Cameras on Police–Citizen Contacts: Findings from a Controlled Experiment in Mesa, AZ." *Journal of Experimental Criminology* 11 (3): 445–458.

Reaves, B. A. 2010. *Local Police Departments, 2007*. Washington, DC: Department of Justice, Bureau of Justice Statistics.

Reiss, A. J. 1973. *The Police and the Public*. Vol. 39. New Haven, CT: Yale University Press.

Roberts, K., and V. Herrington. 2013. "Organisational and Procedural Justice: A Review of the Literature and Its Implications for Policing." *Journal of Policing, Intelligence and Counter Terrorism* 8 (2): 115–130.

Roy, A. 2014. "On-officer Video Cameras: Examining the Effects of Police Department Policy and Assignment on Camera Use and Activation." Unpublished master's thesis. Arizona State University, Tempe, AZ.

Schafer, J. A. 2013. "The Role of Trust and Transparency in the Pursuit of Procedural and Organisational Justice." *Journal of Policing, Intelligence and Counter Terrorism* 8 (2): 131–143.

Srivastava, S. 2009. "Explorations in Police Organisation: An Indian Context." *International Journal of Police Science & Management* 11 (3): 255–273.

Stanley, J. 2014. *The Video Revolution in Policing*. Retrieved October 21, 2014 from American Civil Liberties Union Web site: https://www.aclu.org/

Tankebe, J. 2010. "Identifying the Correlates of Police Organizational Commitment in Ghana." *Police Quarterly* 13 (1): 73–91.

The White House, Office of the Press Secretary. 2015. *FACT SHEET: Strengthening Community Policing*. Washington, DC: The White House.

Thibaut, J., and L. Walker. 1975. *Procedural Justice: A Psychological Analysis*. Hillsdale, NJ: Erlbaum.

Tinker, R., T. R. Tyler, and Goff, P. A. 2016. "Justice from within: The Relations between a Procedurally Just Organizational Climate and Police Organizational Efficiency, Endorsement of Democratic Policing and Officer Well-Being." *Psychology, Public Policy, and Law* 22 (2): 158–172.

Trubek, D. 1972. "Max Weber on Law and the Rise of Capitalism." *Faculty Scholarship Series: Yale Law School, Paper* 4001: 720–752.

Tyler, T. R., P. E. Callahan, and J. Frost. 2007. "Armed, and Dangerous (?): Motivating Rule Adherence among Agents of Social Control." *Law & Society Review* 41 (2): 457–492.

Tyler, T. R., and J. Jackson. 2014. "Popular Legitimacy and the Exercise of Legal Authority: Motivating Compliance, Cooperation, and Engagement." *Psychology, Public Policy, and Law* 20 (1): 78–95.

Tyler, T. R., and J. Sunshine. 2003. "The Role of Procedural Justice and Legitimacy in Shaping Public Support for Policing." *Law & Society Review* 37 (3): 513–548.

White, M. D. 2014. *Police Officer Body-worn Cameras: Assessing the Evidence*. Washington, DC: Office of Community Oriented Policing Services.

Wolfe, S. E., and A. R. Piquero. 2011. "Organizational Justice and Police Misconduct." *Criminal Justice and Behavior* 38 (4): 332–353.

Understanding the culture of craft: lessons from two police agencies

James J. Willis and Stephen D. Mastrofski

ABSTRACT

When it comes to changing American policing, the police culture is invariably a target for reform. However, characterizations of traditional police attitudes and beliefs as suspicious of outsiders, authoritative, and at odds with the law, often overlook what police officers themselves value about the work they do, that is what constitutes its quality. Using survey data from two police departments, this paper seeks to understand the contours of the police craft culture. Our findings suggest a more textured assessment of police culture is warranted than the 'warrior' outlook implies. While some of the views of our respondents were consistent with features of the traditional police culture, officers did not display the kind of cynicism about the public, rush to judgment, preoccupation with coercive tactics, indifference to rules and regulations, and deep skepticism about science consistent with this portrayal of the police. We then consider how these insights might be used by those seeking to improve street-level police work.

Introduction

Over the past year in the United States, video footage of what appeared to be fairly routine encounters between police officers and members of the public has raised significant concerns about troublesome police practices that have, on occasion, delivered tragic outcomes. The ensuing public outcry about police abuse of authority and mistreatment, especially of black citizens, has provoked national debate, and similar to past reform efforts the 'police culture' has been identified as a major impediment to improvements in American policing (Civil Rights Division, U.S. Department of Justice 2015; Rahr and Rice 2015).

The culture of policing is a popular target for those promoting reforms that require a change in the philosophy and methods of street-level police work, where the culture is thought to reside. Advocates of community policing, problem-oriented policing, procedural justice, and evidence-based policing have anticipated resistance from the police culture, and studies have examined the difficulties in overcoming these challenges to reform (Weisburd and Braga 2006). Moreover, the police culture is frequently cited by top police executives as needing change in their own departments (Mastrofski 2015). The most recent, highly visible document advocating reform highlights changing police culture as a central element in the reformers' pathway to successfully changing police practices (President's Task Force 2015). And yet, it is not entirely clear that the orthodox view of the police culture first developed in the 1950s is an accurate characterization of how officers orient themselves to their work today. That view has been summarized as police sharing a suspicious attitude, being sensitive to challenges to their authority, experiencing isolation from the public, and cleaving to an extreme loyalty toward fellow officers (National Research Council 2004, 130–133). More recently, these features have been characterized as a militaristic culture (Rahr and Rice 2015).

But the police culture may not be so uniform as contemporary reformers and the pioneering police ethnographers claimed (Banton 1964; Skolnick 1966; Westley 1970; Rubinstein 1973; Van Maanen 1974; Manning 1977; Fielding 1984), and various forces afoot in the selection, training, and socialization process may be reshaping the culture or producing a more variegated condition of competing subcultures (Paoline 2001). Some note the possibility that the police culture may be changing in ways that make it more receptive to *au courant* reforms (Sklansky 2006), while others find evidence of little change (Loftus 2009). Regardless, the cultural orientations of police workers remain a major apprehension of those intent on transforming police performance (Campeau 2015).

Given this widespread concern, it is striking that those wishing to change the culture have not paid more attention to what officers value about the work itself – what constitutes its *quality*, how best to achieve it, and how best to avoid low quality. In comparison to police attitudes toward other prominent features of the working environment, such as the police role and views toward the public, patrol officers' views on the craft elements of their work remain understudied. Much of our understanding about officers' conceptions of the police craft continues to stem from studies conducted decades ago, and Herbert's (1998, 358) observation that craft, or the 'normative order of competence,' was the least understood of police officers' cultural outlooks still pertains today.

Using survey data collected in two police departments, this paper addresses this lacuna. We seek to develop a clearer understanding of the contours of the police culture of craft, including the level of agreement on who the high performers of patrol work are, the goals that define good policing, the causes of undesirable results, the most important craft skills, and how to judge quality when assessing police performance. In doing so we ask, 'To what extent do officers' conceptions of high quality police work comport with currently popular and earlier accounts of the police craft, and are there new developments that need to be taken into account?' The answer to this question is important as an empirically grounded understanding of how the workers conceive what 'doing a good job' means can provide valuable insights into the kinds of reforms that are both pressing and possible for improving police performance (Thacher 2008).

The police occupational culture and the culture of craft

Based on ethnographic research on routine police work, an influential perspective on occupation-centric views of police officers emerged in the 1950s (Westley 1953, 1956) and blossomed in the 1960s and 1970s (Skolnick 1966; Wilson 1968; Rubinstein 1973; Van Maanen 1974; Reiner 1978), becoming known as the 'police culture' (Reiner 1985; Chan 1996; O'Neill, Marks, and Singh 2007; Paoline and Terrill 2014). Researchers noted the presence of informal norms, beliefs, and priorities among the police, often at odds with the formal expectations articulated in laws and regulations and ostensibly enforced by department hierarchies, courts, and other institutions (Chan 2007, 339). This literature identified common aspects of the police work environment (danger, coercive authority, hierarchical scrutiny, and role ambiguity) contributing to officer work stress. This yielded widespread coping strategies (suspiciousness, controlling behavior, maintaining low visibility, and seeking validation as a law enforcer or crime fighter), with outcomes such as isolation from outsiders and intense solidarity with one's fellow officers (Paoline 2004). Other features of the occupational culture included conservative politics and morality, the celebration of a strong masculine perspective valorizing courage, honor, and strength, and cynicism about people and their motives (Loftus 2010, 1; Cockcroft 2013). Although elements of craft surface in this characterization of a monolithic police culture, these have not been central to understanding police perspectives on the nature of the work they do.

Research since the 1980s has challenged this view of a universally shared set of values, focusing on how much police culture has been fragmented into different subcultures within police departments (Paoline 2003; Mastrofski and Willis 2010, 100). A number of these studies have identified different styles of policing based on variation in the outlooks of officers within the same police department using many of the same cultural dimensions identified decades earlier (see Worden 1995 and Paoline 2003 for useful overviews). In constructing typologies of different officer styles (e.g., street cop versus management cop, reactors versus tough cops), craft is sometimes mentioned but it is a marginal consideration in understanding officers' orientations toward their work (Reuss-Ianni 1983; Mastrofski, Willis, and Snipes 2002). For example, Brown (1981) examines how officers prioritize the work they consider worth doing ('selectivity') and Paoline, Myers, and Worden (2000) give consideration to how police officers assign value to different kinds of work associated with community policing and the traditional enforcement approach. However, in both cases, these conceptualizations are only tangentially related to craft. Other than Muir (1977), Bayley and Bittner (1984), and Herbert (1998), it is fair to say that within this subcultural approach, research on the craft aspects of police work is not well developed.

With this portraiture, researchers have illuminated a number of specific police views and practices as constituting an occupational perspective on competence or craft in police work, focusing mostly on patrol. Researchers have continued to explore the cultural implications of new organizational strategies over the last two decades, but much less is known about how patrol officers think about the substance of the work they do. It is to this characterization of work competence that we turn.

Policing has long been viewed as a craft, whose members 'think of themselves as set apart from society, possessors of an art that can be learned only by experience' (Wilson 1968, 283). Egon Bittner (1983, 3) referred to it as 'workmanship' and identified aspects of street-level patrol work highly valued by practitioners as the 'resources of knowledge, skill, and judgment to meet and master the unexpected within one's sphere of competence.' These capture much of what other researchers have imputed to traditional craft culture, so we use them here as an organizing base.

Knowledge

Bayley and Bittner (1984) claim that the accomplishment of certain goals frames the occupation's understanding of skilled police work: meeting department norms, containing violence and controlling disorder, preventing crime, avoiding physical injury, and not provoking the public to retaliate in career-threatening ways. Meeting department goals can involve meeting productivity expectations (calls answered, citations, and arrests), accomplishing the leadership's priorities, or conforming to bureaucratic mechanisms designed to shape how officers exercise their discretion (Reiss 1992). Related to the department goal of productivity, though often expressed and enforced through informal channels, is the importance of handling one's share of the workload (Reuss-Ianni 1983; Herbert 1998, 359). Expectations expressed through official policies impose constraints on what officers can do (e.g., arrest for minor offenses), and are regarded as unhelpful as they are often not 'clearly expressed or understood' (Bayley and Bittner 1984, 40).

Maintaining or restoring peace is also a valued goal, which justifies a central tenet of street competence: preserving control (Manning 1977). This justifies police protecting their authority, brooking neither resistance nor disrespect from the public (Bittner 1974; Muir 1977). In addition, minimizing the risk of physical injury to oneself and other officers has been observed as the most frequently articulated value among street officers (Herbert 1998, 375). Extremes of unnecessary escalation and avoidance of danger are frowned upon as unacceptable degradations or derelictions of duty.

The traditional view of the police culture also places high value on the acquisition of detailed knowledge of particular people and places where the officer works – which amounts to intimate awareness of the 'physical ecology,' 'local culture' (Fielding 1984, 575), and the history of events (Bittner 1967). This requires both passive observation of the patterns of life in an assigned area, as well as actively getting to know the regulars who live, work, and play there, both by talking to them and indirectly through other sources (Bittner 1967).

Skills

Certain skills also frequently surface in accounts of police competence (Wilson 1968, 32). Adeptness with weapons, physical fitness, and martial arts are mentioned, particularly as manifestations of masculinity and drama (Manning 1977; Miller 1999), but researchers note that officers pay homage to peers who by their mere visibility and demeanor find ways to calm situations and prevent problems (Fielding 1984, 57). Even more frequently, researchers report that the traditional culture values verbal skills that minimize the need for physical exertion or the assertion of formal authority by instead manipulating persons by other means, such as questioning, threatening, persuading, or negotiating (Bittner 1967; 711; Fielding 1984, 570; Muir 1977). This softer and less cynical side of policing is often downplayed in characterizations of the traditional police culture (e.g., Niederhoffer 1967), but we note the presence of a more complex set of craft values that are intertwined with harder views of the police culture.

Judgment

Finally, because patrol work is 'fraught with decision' (Bayley and Bittner 1984, 36), police craft emphasizes the importance of sorting through the information available in a given situation that can be troublesome and dynamic, processing it, and forming judgments about what is happening (Muir 1977; ch. 10). How to identify relevant indicia, how to elicit additional information that is reliable, and how to process and evaluate the pattern of available information – all go into the diagnostic process. Ethnographers often comment upon the apparent crudeness of diagnostic categories street officers use to govern their choices (e.g., governable versus ungovernable) (Muir 1977), but they also describe the complexities of recognizing relevant cues, analyzing the situation, and the subtlety and skill required to produce accurate judgments (Bittner 1967; Kelling 1999). Rather than the kind of snap judgments heavily influenced by intuition and emotion, this form of decision-making more closely resembles the kind of effortful, reasoned, and deliberative process captured by cognitive approaches such as 'reflection-in-action' (Schon 1983) and System II thinking (Kahneman 2011). A key component of these approaches is the selection of a feasible resolution of the situation from available alternatives.

These claims of the nature of the traditional police craft were offered more than three decades ago, well before the many reforms intending to alter the police culture had an opportunity to have an effect. Knowing how, if at all, dispositions of the craft view of competence and quality in police work have changed is a necessary first step for considering how these might inform reform efforts to improve street-level performance. Before turning to how much of the traditional police culture is revealed by delving into police attitudes toward work competence in two police agencies, we discuss our research sites and methods.

Research sites

This research was conducted in two police agencies, Everdene and Newbury (pseudonyms). These sites were selected because the research team had previously worked with these agencies in various ways and enjoyed the confidence of the department leadership. Everdene, a department of approximately 100 officers, serves a suburban community, half who are minority. Approximately one in ten residents falls below the poverty line; the violent crime rate is slightly above average for its population size. Newbury, an urban area with suburban developments, has approximately three times Everdene's number of officers and a violent crime well below average for communities of its size. A third of the population is minority; about 10% of residents are below the poverty line. Everdene and Newbury were similar in their policing approach. Both showed commitment to community policing, working in close partnership with residents and businesses to identify and solve neighborhood problems. Both valued community-oriented job applicants and assigned such specialists to engage in public outreach.

It is hazardous to generalize from two police agencies, and we make no claim that Everdene and Newbury are representative of the thousands of police departments in the United States. Nonetheless, when we compare Everdene and Newbury to their peers, they appear to be in the mainstream of contemporary American local police departments on many dimensions –based on the 2013 Law Enforcement Management and Administrative Survey of 2,353 local police departments in the United States (Reaves 2015). Both departments have sworn staffing at the national average, have minimal education requirements (high school) that are typical of the vast majority of American departments, and incorporate community policing into their mission statements, as do the majority of agencies nationwide, and especially in their size range. Both departments do have a larger portion of officers who are female (especially Everdene), and Everdene has a higher percentage of minority police officers. Aside from officer demographics, on all other available indicators they are close to or consistent with the majority of either the national sample or their respective population subgroups. Everdene and Newbury are not outliers, falling well within the bounds of what is normal. Because their leadership, like that of so many others, had responded positively to many of the currently popular reforms that seek to alter the culture of police, they are interesting and appropriate sites for our study.

Research methods

Questionnaires were administered to patrol officers at roll call and other convenient occasions in the Everdene and Newbury Police Departments in 2010 and 2012, respectively. These surveys were part of a larger project that took time to acquire other data in each department with a small research staff, accounting for the interval between the two surveys. The vast majority of questionnaires were completed and returned on the occasion that they were handed out, but a few respondents completed the surveys later and mailed them to us in postage-paid envelopes. Eighty-eight Everdene patrol officers were eligible to receive the survey. Of the 68 surveys distributed, 82% were completed and returned in Everdene ($N = 56$). In Newbury there were 165 eligible personnel; 118 were available, and 114 of them returned completed surveys (97%). Those officers we were unable to reach were off duty, training, vacationing, or on sick leave when the survey was distributed. These sorts of absences are routine rotations, and there is no reason to expect that they introduced bias into the sample. A summary of respondent characteristics is shown in Table 1. The largest portion of respondents at both sites were patrol-rank officers with 10 or more years of experience, and 2 years or more of college.

Because we were interested in what qualities distinguished officers among their peers as craftspeople, the questionnaire asked respondents to identify the two officers currently in the department (other than themselves) whom they considered to be at the top in performance of patrol officer duties. They were instructed to consider officers of any rank and in any unit, but they were to focus on their abilities to perform patrol officer responsibilities. This follows the methodology employed by Bayley and Garofalo (1989), who used surveys to get New York City police officers to identify officers whom they considered particularly skilled at handling conflict situations in citizen encounters.[1] On our anonymous questionnaire, respondents were asked to identify the best performer and then the next best performer. For each

Table 1. Characteristics of survey respondents in Everdene and Newbury departments.

Characteristics		Everdene (%)	Newbury (%)
Rank	Patrol officer	70	82
	Sergeant	13	7
	Above Sergeant	17	11
Years as a police officer	Less than 3 years	13	15
	3–6 years	27	30
	7–9 years	9	16
	10 years or more	51	39
Highest level of education	High school	13	7
	Some college but less than baccalaureate	40	46
	Baccalaureate degree	24	35
	Some graduate school/law school	13	6
	Graduate or law degree	11	7

Note: Percentages may not sum to 100 due to rounding error.

officer identified, respondents were asked to describe the features of that officer's performance that most impressed the respondent (open-ended question). Respondents were assured that the names of persons they identified would not be disclosed. The questionnaire then asked respondents to give their views on aspects of evaluating patrol officers' performance, priorities in different field situations in which police engage the public, the quality of police work, and personal characteristics of the respondent.

Findings

Top performers and their distinguishing features

Consistent with portrayals of the traditional police culture (Bayley and Bittner 1984; Bayley and Garofalo 1989), we found that respondents' selection of high performing officers converged disproportionately on a relative small number of officers. In Everdene, 11 of the department's 88 officers (or 12.5% of the force) accounted for 63.7% of the 91 nominations made by survey respondents. Similarly, in Newbury, 15 of the department's 313 officers (or 4.8% of the force) accounted for 48% of the top performer nominations. The consensus was not overwhelming, but in the views of the Everdene and Newbury police, the highest quality performance was clearly concentrated in a relatively small group of officers.[2] The degree of reputational concentration observed in these departments is all the more remarkable, given the fragmented nature of the work, where opportunities to observe large numbers of other officers directly at work are limited by the confinements of stable work shifts and geographically dispersed assignments.

In both agencies, approximately nine of ten respondents indicated that they were most influenced in their selection by their direct observations of the identified officers at work. Only a small portion of officers indicated other sources, such as hearing second-hand from other officers. Contrary to the claim that police reputations (in large departments) are easily constructed by second-hand accounts of one's actions and accomplishments (Van Maanen 1974; Muir 1977), officers in these smaller departments relied overwhelmingly on what they themselves observed directly.

In contrast to the high level of consensus on individuals identified as top performers, there was greater diversity on what distinguished these individuals to deserve that assessment. Classifying respondents' characterizations of the features of the officers' performance that most impressed them yielded 13 categories that clustered conceptually, often with multiple characteristics mentioned for each top performer.[3] Table 2 shows the distribution of responses according to the categories that emerged, taking the characterizations of all officers who were named into account.

In both departments (especially Everdene), the most frequently mentioned characterization of top performing officers was having good work habits, habits that one would expect to see admired in any human service bureaucracy. These included being a hard worker, attentive to details, disciplined, follows

Table 2. Most impressive features of top performing officers.

Features	Everdene (%)	Newbury (%)
Work habits	76.9	55.8
Eloquence, interpersonal skills, work with community	55.8	37.7
Knowledge/Experience	50.0	55.2
Judgment	50.0	22.1
Leader/helpful	48.1	29.2
Demeanor	25.0	16.2
Investigator	21.2	7.8
General skills	19.2	16.2
Misc. abilities	19.2	17.5
Safety habits	13.5	17.8
Fair/impartial	13.5	6.5
Physical/martial arts	11.5	2.6
Writing/reports	9.6	5.8

Note: Percentages indicate proportion of respondents who mentioned this feature at least once. Percentages across categories exceed 100, because respondents often provided multiple features for each person they identified.

orders, positive attitude, reliable, shows initiative, does not complain, and productive activity levels. Knowledge (including education and training) and experience also ranked high on desirable traits across both agencies (mentioned by at least 1 in 2 officers), as did the ability to speak well (including interpersonal skills, public relations, explains decisions). However, Everdene officers afforded greater emphasis to judgment (including good decision-making and tactical choices, diagnostic/observation skills, handles stressful situations well, creative problem solver, and common sense) and being a good leader (including being a good instructor, helpful to others, uses a team approach) than officers in Newbury. Demeanor included fitting deportment to the situation, being calm, and showing a command presence. Fair/impartial also included not being swayed by pleasing the public. Some skill character-izations were too general to classify with specificity ('skilled,' 'professional,' or 'the best') and so were assigned to the general skills category. Miscellaneous abilities included responses not covered by any of the other categories.

In both agencies, items that figure prominently in many popular depictions of policing and academic accounts of traditional police culture (safety, physical shape/martial arts, and investigative skills) were infrequent. It could be that officers felt that these were very important, but that there was not much variation among peers. Consequently, these would be features that officers would not use to select those who rose above the rest.

The table shows officers emphasize some traits that are consistent with well-established views of the police occupational culture (e.g., appreciating good workers, acknowledging the worth of knowl-edge, experience, and eloquence), but it also shows that reformers may have exaggerated its 'warrior' aspects (Rahr and Rice 2015). When it came to selecting high performers, the officers in our sample stressed reliability and 'brain work.' They did not simply identify traits consistent with crime fighting, toughness, and danger. Stylizing police culture by overstating these aspects deflects attention from a more nuanced and sophisticated understanding of the philosophies, abilities, and methods of these high performers or craftspeople.

The importance of different performance: the traffic violation and the domestic dispute

Knowing what set the high-reputation officers apart from all others helps illuminate what is at the pinna-cle of the value system of Everdene and Newbury officers, but the picture is incomplete. To comprehend the structure of that value system more fully, we explored the relative importance of a variety of goals that patrol officers might embrace. Consequently, we asked respondents to consider two scenarios, a traffic violation and a domestic dispute,[4] and to indicate the level of priority (top, moderate, low, not a priority) of 10 possible performance elements in the quality of an officer's performance. Note that this question addresses something different from what the officer regards as distinctive about the performance of a highly skilled peer. Here, the officer is asked to consider priorities for what requires an officer's attention. It admits to a broader range of influences on the inclination to make those choices.

We selected these two relatively common situations, because other scholars have identified them as particularly problematic or challenging due to uncertainty about whom the officer is dealing with and what the citizen will do (Bayley and Bittner 1984). Performance elements included several goals men-tioned by Bayley and Bittner: safety and order, following rules and legal requirements, and preventing a recurrence of this problem. We also added an item that decades of research have shown figure largely in the police occupational culture: offering punishment or leniency according to the citizen's demeanor (National Research Council 2004, 120). In addition, we added items related to procedural justice (Tyler 2004), an approach that reformers have advocated to improve policing by reducing police-citizen alienation. Procedural justice focuses on how much consideration officers show citizens and includes officers explaining their decisions, showing respect, listening to citizens, and basing a response on facts, not personal feelings. Finally, we included two items that have been suggested as appropriate considerations (Mastrofski 1996): making the response appropriate to the seriousness of the situation, and selecting an efficient response (one that economizes police time and effort). We asked officers to rate each performance element according to the priority it should receive in evaluating the quality of

Table 3. Top performance priorities in traffic and domestic dispute situations.

Priority	Everdene (%)		Newbury (%)	
	Traffic	Domestic	Traffic	Domestic
Maintain safety and order at scene	98.0	100.0	95.6	100.0
Follow rules/laws	83.6	81.5	84.1	83.2
Base response on facts, not feelings	54.5	64.8	78.9	69.0
Match response to seriousness	46.4	55.6	52.6	56.6
Increase future road safety/household peace	36.4	44.4	37.7	66.4
Show respect and listen to citizen	35.7	51.9	39.8	62.5
Explain decision to citizens	23.6	24.8	27.2	37.7
Treat citizens according to attitude	14.5	13.0	12.3	15.9
Reduce future citizen complaints	10.9	3.7	20.2	18.8
Save police time/effort	7.3	5.6	9.6	9.6

an officer's performance. Table 3 shows for each performance element the percentage of respondents indicating that it was a top priority.

Table 3 reveals a strikingly consistent response pattern, whether the situation was a traffic violation or a domestic dispute. One exception was showing respect and listening to citizens. A substantially greater proportion of officers in both departments gave higher priority to this goal in the domestic dispute than the traffic violation. In Newbury, an additional exception to this pattern of shared priorities in disputes and traffic stops was the priority given to reducing the recurrence of the problem in domestics compared to traffic stops. In Newbury, leadership sent a clearer message that mitigating future problems should be a focus of patrol officer attention, which was conveyed in many ways, including a heavy emphasis on the department's version of Compstat to identify and eliminate recurring problems.

The priorities identified by officers reveal some values that are consistent with the traditional police culture, and others not. Maintaining safety and order at the scene are fundamental to the accomplishment of all other objectives and figure prominently in every field account of patrol work since Skolnick's pioneering work (1966). This contrasts sharply with the relatively low number of officers who identified safety habits as a distinguishing feature of the high-performing officers they selected. Our reconciliation of this apparent disjuncture requires speculation. As we noted earlier, it seems apparent that our respondents placed a high value on maintaining safety and order at the scene of these common situations, but it may also be that they perceived little variation on these fundamental skills. They may see most of their peers as quite competent in this regard, and hence are not inclined to select it as distinctive.

Not anticipated from most prior research is the high priority given to following rules and laws. Indeed much of that literature dwells on the tension between satisfying rule-based, legalistic standards and doing what is necessary to accomplish worthy goals, which is either not covered by rules and laws or is in contravention to it (Bittner 1983; Skolnick and Fyfe 1994, 120). The attentiveness of most officers to following rules, though downplayed by much of the literature on police culture, is anticipated by Herbert (1998). He noted the central role that law and bureaucracy played in creating 'normative orders,' or guides for police behavior based on observations of officers in the Los Angeles Police Department in the 1990s, a much larger department than Everdene and Newbury. The ethos of departments can differ, so it remains to be seen how much this varies across a much larger, representative sample of agencies.

Our respondents' attention to legal concerns may simply be a by-product of attempts over the years to impose stricter legal constraints on the resolution of domestic disputes and perhaps is not indicative of a more general shift in attitudes. But the fact that officers also assigned importance to the proper application of regulations and laws in traffic stops suggests that legal considerations could be a more powerful influence on police practices than previously allowed. The obvious implication would be that any attempts to shape police behavior should include stressing formal rules and regulations rather than simply assuming they are impotent.

The organizational pressure for efficiency and productivity that Skolnick first noted (1966) also did not manifest itself in responses to the item asking about the priority given to saving police time and effort.

Furthermore, and in contrast to Bayley and Bittner (1984), officers in these departments did not seem particularly concerned about the potential for future citizen complaints. Few ranked it as a top priority.

Our respondents' craft priorities also do not align easily with a cultural outlook that portrays officers as officious, cynical, and prejudiced by how citizens respond to their authority (Reuss-Ianni 1983, 20–21). In contrast, three procedural justice items (making decisions based on facts not feelings, showing respect and listening to people, and not treating citizens according to their attitude) resonated strongly with our officers, at least in the domestic dispute scenario. In these departments, procedural justice (a police reform highly touted in the President's Task Force report on 21st Century policing) appeared to be an important feature of street-level work. More consistent with the traditional view of the police as suspicious and distrusting of the public was the lower priority officers in Everdene and Newbury assigned to the procedural justice element of explaining their decisions to citizens. This is consistent with other research findings that police may be reluctant to explain their actions, as it opens their decisions to dispute (Jonathan-Zamir, Mastrofski, and Moyal 2015). A fuller expression of procedural justice will likely require convincing these officers of the value in demonstrating neutrality by articulating the reasons for their decisions.

Tactical choices with undesirable results

Although the focus of the survey was identifying aspects of police practice that produce the highest quality work, we did not assume that what produces undesirable outcomes is simply the opposite of what produces desirable outcomes. Consequently, we asked respondents, 'When a patrol officer's decision or actions with the public produce *undesirable* results, which one of the following pairs is more often the cause?'[5] We then presented 11 pairs of options reflecting choices an officer could make in dealing with the public.[6] Respondents chose between too much and too little of the action indicated.

Table 4 displays the pattern of responses for the 11 pairs. The highest level of consensus in Everdene and Newbury (94 and 89%, respectively) was observed for the statement that the officer did not gather information from enough sources, as opposed to too many sources. The item with one of the lowest levels of consensus had to do with toleration of disrespect and there was considerable disagreement on this item across departments. In Everdene, slightly more respondents indicated that undesirable outcomes were more likely when the officer was not sufficiently tolerant of citizen disrespect (54%), while in Newbury, 68% of respondents thought the chances of an undesirable outcome increased when officers were *too* tolerant of citizen disrespect.

Portrayals of the traditional police culture have tended to emphasize the idiosyncratic, reactive, and arbitrary dimensions of officer choice-making in interactions with the public. This is especially true of advocates of evidence-based policing who draw sharp distinctions between objective decision-making rooted in the rigors of empirical science versus the kind of subjective considerations (e.g., personal feelings) that are assumed to influence the craft unduly (Lum 2009, 9; Sherman 2013). More often than

Table 4. Most likely causes of undesirable results in police-citizen interactions.

Cause	Everdene (%)	Newbury (%)
Not enough information sources	94.4	89.0
Did not take enough time	81.8	80.9
Too harsh	80.0	70.6
Not enough explanation to citizens	76.4	74.1
Too lenient	74.1	71.0
Not enough alternatives considered	73.6	77.1
Not follow rules closely	70.9	72.6
Did not follow intuition	70.0	81.3
Authority not asserted soon enough	64.8	77.1
Not enough citizen input	63.6	62.0
Too tolerant of citizen disrespect	46.3	67.6

Note: The percentage of respondents for only the most popular response of each pair (not enough versus too much) is provided, with the exception of the last entry for Everdene, which showed a different pattern than Newbury on that item.

not, the high level of agreement among respondents that a failure to be deliberative is the cause of undesirable results challenges the notion that the decision-making process based on experience stands in firm opposition to the scientific method. Indeed, three items on which 74% or more of the officers agreed share with the evidence-based policing movement's concern with using reason and careful observation to guide action: not seeking information from enough sources, not taking enough time overall to deal with the situation, and not considering enough alternatives to solve the problem. While intuition does continue to play an important role in street-level choices, officers' responses suggest a much richer decision process than succumbing to the pressure to make snap decisions. The value respondents placed on *both* intuitive and deliberative decision might seem paradoxical, but it likely implies that officers are distinguishing between the advantages of systematically gathering information and using intuition to interpret that information and translate it into a judgment.

Generally consistent with the performance priorities respondents identified in traffic and domestic dispute was the degree to which procedural justice seemed to be present in officers' judgments: over 70% indicated that being too harsh was more likely to produce undesirable results and around 6 out of 10 officers agreed that not allowing enough input from the citizens involved was a problem. In a time when reformers urge police to embrace procedural justice, there appears to be at least acceptance of it in Everdene and Newbury. That officers should rate the *absence* of procedural justice as a frequent cause of difficulties can be contrasted with the comparatively lower frequency with which this sample named procedural justice items as top priorities in traffic enforcement and domestic dispute situations (see Table 3). This is especially true when it comes to explaining one's actions to citizens: here about three quarters of officers say insufficient explanation is the more likely cause of a problem (compared to too much explanation), while in the earlier table only about a quarter of respondents regarded explanations to citizens as important.

This suggests that the positive and negative aspects of performance are not necessarily mirrored reverses of each other. This probably reflects the traditional 'cover-your-ass' perspective that problems and trouble tend to come to officers from outside their own informal value system – the department's disciplinary apparatus, the press, and the public. Rather than being recognized for doing something well, patrol officers understand that they are more likely to be recognized 'for something they have done wrong' (Paoline, Myers, and Worden 2006, 578).

Table 4 also contains an apparent contradiction between officers identifying too much leniency and too much severity (the officer was too harsh) as more often than not the cause of undesirable consequences. This might be indicating that officers believe poor judgment is the culprit, or an inability to fashion a police severity of response that is appropriate to the situation.

Taken as a whole, eight of the paired choices produced consensus above 70% in both departments, focusing primarily on the need for officers to be more deliberative and to attend to procedural justice issues. The former suggests a craft culture that valorizes a more sophisticated approach to decision-making than usually recognized while the latter suggests a police culture that may be adapting to new demands in the police environment. The high degree of agreement on the items related to procedural justice coupled with a lack of consensus between officers in Everdene and in Newbury on when to assert one's authority and how much citizen disrespect to tolerate might suggest that officers are becoming more sensitive (and perhaps equivocal) about managing the tension between exercising coercion over people while simultaneously treating them positively.

Skills and knowledge that promote good police performance

Notwithstanding their differences, a shared vision of recent reform attempts is officers' reliance on technology and empirical inquiry to diagnose and treat problems of crime and disorder. For problem-oriented policing, the officer is a 'neighborhood clinician' (Goldstein 1990), and under evidence-based policing, scientific evidence should be the foundation of police discretion (Sherman 2015). To what extent did these concerns coincide with respondents' views of the skills and knowledge that promote good police performance? To answer this, we asked respondent to rate the importance of 13 different

Table 5. Average rating of skills and knowledge promoting good police performance

Skills/Knowledge	Everdene		Newbury	
	Mean	(s.d.)	Mean	(s.d.)
Laws, rules, and regulations	4.95	(.23)	4.93	(.26)
People, places, and customs	4.31	(.74)	4.46	(.72)
Negotiation	4.27	(.68)	4.32	(.75)
Verbal coercion	4.24	(.79)	4.27	(.76)
Defensive tactics	4.13	(.79)	4.46	(.69)
Writing	4.13	(.75)	4.11	(.76)
Physical fitness	4.09	(.76)	4.37	(.79)
Persuasion	4.11	(.74)	4.34	(.73)
Public speaking	4.00	(.79)	3.96	(.87)
Good relations with community leaders	3.76	(.88)	3.66	(1.07)
Computers and information technology	3.53	(.74)	3.64	(.80)
Crime analysis	3.22	(.79)	3.46	(1.03)
Scientific evidence on what works	3.15	(1.01)	3.35	(.86)

Note: 5 = very important, 4 = important, 3 = somewhat important; 2 = a little important; 1 = not at all important.

skills or knowledge areas on a five-point scale. We selected these items because some had long been a core part of the training and development protocols of professional departments (for example, knowledge of the law and physical fitness), while others have emerged more recently (use of scientific knowledge, crime analysis). Still others are frequently mentioned by police leaders as invaluable, but are often learned on the job (e.g., knowledge of people and places and skills in persuasion, negotiation, and verbal coercion).

Table 5 shows the average response (on a five-point scale) for each of the items. Consistent with our earlier finding of the high priority most officers give to following laws and rules, the sample almost uniformly rated the knowledge of laws, rules, and regulations pertaining to the officer's duties as very important. Almost as important were knowledge of people, places, and customs. Also noteworthy was the relatively strong showing of various interpersonal and communication skills, which were generally rated in the same 'important' range as martial arts and combativeness that have traditionally been mentioned as part of the macho, adventure-oriented culture of officers (Herbert 1998). Perhaps most conspicuous were the weaker showings of technological, scientific, and analytic skills. Knowledge of scientific evidence, the bedrock of the evidence-based policing movement, averaged in the 'somewhat important' range. This might be predicted by those who note the lower level of respect accorded science as a policing skill (Bayley and Bittner 1984; Weisburd and Neyroud 2011), but it is still above the scale's midpoint and thus reflective of a much greater receptivity than is sometimes credited (Telep and Lum 2014). Also rated lower were the political skills that are highly valued in community policing, a reform that these departments featured as key to their service to their jurisdictions.

Much of what respondents identified as important about skills and knowledge needed for good performance has long been considered part of police culture. A fine-grained knowledge of people and places is considered essential to good police work, as is verbal facility. However, similar to our findings about the features that distinguish high-performing officers, the importance respondents accorded to communication and interpersonal skills tempers the entrenched view of an occupational culture steeped in toughness and aggression. Less consistent with the traditional police culture, as we have remarked elsewhere, was the priority our officers assigned to understanding laws and rules as features of high-quality police work.

Judging patrol officer performance

In judging patrol officer performance, departments have traditionally given priority to activities, not outcomes (Rubinstein 1973, 41), leading officers to play the 'numbers game' of making arrests, conducting field investigations, and issuing citations in order to receive positive appraisals from their superiors (Skolnick and Fyfe 1994, 126). In contrast, patrol officers themselves are disinclined to identify productivity as a feature of good police work. Given this tension, we were curious about how much importance respondents would give to the *quality* of work performed versus compared to the *quantity*. Consequently we asked, 'When a patrol officer's work performance is evaluated, how much weight should be given to the quantity of work perform as opposed to the quality of work performed.' Table 6 shows that approximately two-thirds of respondents in both departments indicated that less weight should be given to quantity than quality; only 7% preferred that more weight be given to quantity than quality.

While the quality of an officer's performance was the dominant consideration for most officers, large portions also noted the complexity of making judgments about quality. Under many contemporary reforms, such as Compstat and community policing, there is a great deal of pressure on police officers to produce results, whether in the form of arrests, citations, or satisfied citizens (Willis, Mastrofski, and Weisburd 2007). That is, there is an overwhelming emphasis on judging the success of police work by the ends, not the means. We asked officers which was the better indicator of police performance, either the outcomes of the situation handled by the officer, or the decisions made in the situations handled by the officer. The overwhelming response (87% in Everdene and 78% in Newbury) was to focus on the decisions made by the officer in the situation. Most officers selected process over outcome, certainly an expectation consistent with long-established characterizations of the rank-and-file perspective of the need for evaluating performance on a situation-by-situation basis (Kelling 1999, 43–44).

We also wanted to learn what the police craft taught officers about *how* to go about making judgments about work quality in difficult situations. Thus, we asked officers to indicate to what extent they agreed that there were not many general principles promoting good policing, that it is hard to judge officer performance when not on scene, and that a tactic that works well for one officer will probably work well for other officers. Table 7 shows that officers in both departments were divided over whether there were many general principles useful in promoting good policing. What constitutes good policing depends on the particular situation. And only a bit more than a third of officers in both departments agreed that tactics that work well for one officer will probably work well for most. Hence, we observe a fairly widespread sentiment that it is difficult to generalize beyond the particulars of a situation and the officer in assessing police work. Further, a substantial majority (over 70%) felt that making judgments about an officer's performance required being on scene.

Thus, while quality may be 'job one' in the eyes of most respondents, many seem to feel that a simple system for defining and monitoring it is difficult. This may account for the substantial segment of officers who rated their department's formal performance appraisal process as poor or very poor. Forty-three percent of Everdene's officers and 40% of Newbury's rated their department's formal performance appraisal process as poor or very poor in accurately assessing patrol officers' performance *quality* (table not shown). This was much more than the percentage that gave a 'poor/very poor' rating

Table 6. When evaluating performance, how much weight should patrol officers' give quantity versus quality of work performed?

Quantity vs. Quality	Everdene (%)	Newbury
Less weight to quantity	66.1	61.1
Equal weight to quantity and quality	26.8	31.9
More weight to quantity	7.2	7.1

Table 7. Dealing with difficult situations involving members of the public.

	Everdene (%)			Newbury (%)		
How to judge work quality	Agree	Disagree	Undecided	Agree	Disagree	Undecided
Not many general principles for promoting good policing	52.7	38.2	9.1	39.8	42.5	17.7
Good tactic works well for most officers	34.5	45.4	20.0	36.3	48.6	15.0
Must be on scene to judge performance	74.5	20.0	5.5	71.7	23.9	4.4

to the department's system for assessing the *quantity* of patrol officers' performance (23.5% in Everdene and 24.5% in Newbury).

Ethnographers have long noted the importance patrol officers assign to the quality of work they do in assessing performance and the lower value they assign to the usually available statistics (e.g., arrests). Officers' responses in Everdene and Newbury suggest that from a craft perspective, this feature of good police work has changed little since the studies of the 1960s and 1970s. Unlike many reformers and researchers, officers continue to pay close attention to assessing policing processes, not outcomes, within the context of a particular encounter. This is unsurprising, because officers can far more easily control how they behave than they can the ensuing consequences.

Discussion and conclusion

Recent events continue to put the police in the national spotlight, and it has become commonplace to single out the police culture as inimical to the democratic values of individual liberty, dignity, and community trust. Viewed as too eager to enforce the law and assert their authority, the police are portrayed as warriors in combat with ordinary people rather than guardians who serve and protect them (Rahr and Rice 2015, 7). However, our case studies of the Everdene and Newbury police departments suggest a more textured assessment of police culture is warranted, one that better captures what patrol officers themselves value about their work.

To be sure, some of the views of our respondents were consistent with features of the traditional police culture: subscribing to the importance of maintaining safety and order, not shirking work or responsibilities, acquiring detailed situational knowledge through experience, and verbal facility. But at the same time, they did not display the kind of cynicism about the public, rush to judgment, preoccupation with coercive tactics, indifference to rules and regulations, and deep skepticism about science that the warrior label implies. Our findings suggest that these less flattering traits may be overstated and that there are aspects of the police craft culture which scholars and reformers might wish to consider in their attempts to improve street-level policing. In what follows, we focus on these more salutary aspects of the craft culture and their general implications. Obviously, we cannot make strong claims based on findings from only two police agencies, and we acknowledge that meaningful change would require larger changes in organizational structures to support new initiatives. These caveats notwithstanding, some of what we find might be instructive to reformers interested in reshaping police organizations. After all, reforms are more likely to be implemented successfully when they can be harnessed to existing values and beliefs broadly supportive of reformers' goals and principles.

To begin, our officers seemed positively disposed toward many of the requirements of procedural justice, one of the six pillars for improving policing identified by the President's Task Force on twenty-first century policing. Significant majorities of officers indicated that failing to attend to procedural justice matters (especially demeanor, respect, and allowing citizens to have input) were more likely causes of problems for officers. One plausible explanation for this finding is that procedural justice reform engages with the craft mindset we observed because it focuses on the processes (rather than outcomes) of police work. Moreover, these are processes that a police officer can control by deciding to do things differently.

Given craft's focus on how the particularities of any given situation powerfully shape decision-making, the challenge for reformers is telling patrol officers what to do under different circumstances. It will also be important for researchers to measure the downside to any of these tactical specifications. For example, can scientists show there are no side effects to engaging in procedural justice that substantially increase the risk of officer safety? The strong reluctance of officers to generalize principles of good practice, to need to be on scene to judge an officer's performance, and to value processes over outcomes, also helps explain why our respondents were less enthusiastic about reforms such as evidence-based policing. Unlike craft knowledge, scientific knowledge focuses not on distinguishing the particularities and subtleties of a situation and its actors, but rather grasping the features of the situation that allow for an application of general principles for best action and general skills for how to act. Science judges from the distant 'high ground' of research theory and technical rationality, but craft thrives in the immediacy of 'the swampy lowland where situations are confusing messes' (Schon 1983, 42). Furthermore, police science tends to focus on outcomes such as crime control or crime prevention that lacks salience in light of the everyday tasks that tend to occupy an officer's day, namely how to best handle disputes with little risk of violence, social disorder, and minor violations (Telep 2016; Willis and Mastrofski 2016). Finally, we note that these officers did not reject the scientific method, inasmuch as large numbers endorsed taking the time to make observations and reasoning to make inferences about a situation, but they were less enthused about abstract findings, gathered by researchers from afar.

Given these differences, it would seem that to convince officers to adopt evidence-based practices (or a community policing ethos), they must experience the benefits of science-based decision-making directly. If scientific research can readily identify some choices that are better to make than others in terms of producing desirable outcomes, proponents of evidence-based policing should consider training officers well in a given procedure. They could then give officers the opportunity to try it in order to experience the presumed benefits directly. Part of the training should include a systematic discussion of these field experiences among the peer group. This would require careful selection of process measures that concern the street officer for a given procedure, but it could also include outcome measures, too. This could be incorporated into recruit field training and would help personalize the statistical aspects of science by allowing an officer to learn from his/her own pre- and post- performance statistics following the implementation of the tactical change. If seeing is believing for the police, then researchers and police administrators need to help officers see first-hand what science suggests works best.

Of course, if officers in other departments are similarly committed to our respondents' emphasis on the importance of rules and regulations for governing decision-making, it might simply be possible to effect change by incorporating reform practices into existing department policies and exhorting officers to embrace them, along with the implementation of an effective system to monitor performance and reward it. Our respondents were more responsive to formal policy than is widely expected, placing high value on adhering to rules and laws in the traffic stop and domestic dispute scenarios, and there was near unanimity in identifying laws, rules, and regulation as key to *promoting* high quality work. Still, given our respondents' firm belief in observing the success of a given policing approach firsthand, it does not seem that a policy-based approach is likely to be as effective as an approach based on personal experimentation.

Body-worn cameras offer another opportunity for improving street-level performance in ways that are most likely to be embraced from the craft perspective. Since officers care about the specific context of an individual incident and the importance of 'being there' to make meaningful judgments, body-worn camera video footage offers an opportunity for departments to address this cultural feature of the police craft directly. Rather than merely threatening officers with 'gotcha' accountability, the videos could be invaluable for helping officers see what works and what does not. Indeed, such footage could serve as a means for craft practitioners to hold their superiors to account for deficiencies in rules, guidelines, and training.

Currently, police departments have few, if any, formal mechanisms for the systematic sharing of the best knowledge that craft has to offer. Given what we heard, we can envision a more concerted attempt to build a learning environment in police departments that is similar to how hospitals seek to improve the quality of health care through physician peer review (Edwards and Benjamin 2009). Doctors who come across challenging patient cases present the details of these cases to their peers, including the decisions they made and why they made them. These cases then provide a basis for discussion which can lead to articulating key lessons learned and suggestions for how similar cases might be approached in the future. Police departments might consider doing something similar; that is enabling patrol officers to use their body-worn camera footage to present detailed facts on an incident they found especially challenging, paying particular attention to how they diagnosed the nature of the problem and the reasons for their choices. Those considered master craftspeople could be asked to assess the officers' actions and provide constructive feedback on key dimensions of performance. In addition, researchers could be invited to share insights based on the scientific literature. Such a case-based approach might help broaden and strengthen the craft culture's commitment in an agency to careful observation and deliberation in making decisions (Thacher 2001). Furthermore, over time similar cases could provide the basis for deriving general principles that could then be subject to scientific testing before being incorporated into department policies for offering guidance.

If this study were replicated in a large number of diverse departments, we might learn the extent to which our departments' cultural patterns are representative, and the features of police departments and their communities that might account for variation in these patterns. At this stage, we can only note that we found two agencies that in many respects do not fit the popular characterization of the work environment for the patrol function.

Another limitation of this study is that we are unable to determine the influence of the top performers on those who nominated them. Are the top performers nominated merely because they serve as a mirror, reflecting the nominator's own skills, practices, and values, or are they nominated because the nominator views them as a model worthy of emulation, a model they strive to replicate? Developing a deeper understanding of the extent to which the top performers lead, as opposed to being mere tokens of the officers' own self-regard, would be especially useful for police administrators seeking to shape the direction of the culture of craft.

Notes

1. Bayley and Garofalo asked for three names 'to guard against partners being named exclusively' (1984, 4). Everdene and Newbury patrol officers normally work in one-officer units, so we asked for only two names.
2. Our pattern of results is similar to that observed by Bayley and Garofalo (1989, 4), who found that the maximum number of votes any officer received was seldom more than eight.
3. A coding protocol to classify responses was created for each category. A sample of the graduate student's coding was checked by one of the authors for consistency. Questionable codings and ambiguous responses were discussed and resolved.
4. Officers were presented with the following: 'Please think about the sorts of situations in which a patrol officer pulls over a driver for a *traffic violation*, such as speeding. We would like to get your view on the importance of several potential performance elements in this situation. We recognize that each situation is different, so please focus on the most typical situation. For each item below, please indicate what priority it should receive in evaluating the quality of an officer's performance.' Next officers were asked: 'Now please think about a *domestic dispute* between two people where no violence has occurred, but people are upset. We recognize that each situation is different, so please focus on the most typical situation. For each item below, please indicate what priority it should receive in evaluating the quality of an officer's performance.'
5. Undesirable was left to the officer to decide. The particulars of what is undesirable is unimportant for our purposes.
6. These options were drawn from the literature on police culture and decision-making. Intolerance of disrespect, punitiveness, assertion of authority, maintaining control, and following intuition are well documented as powerful policing tendencies. Several items were drawn from the procedural justice literature on soliciting citizen input (Tyler 2004). Muir (1977) and Bayley and Bittner (1984) write about careful diagnoses, which includes taking time and gathering information.

References

Banton, Michael. 1964. *The Policeman in the Community*. New York: Basic Books.

Bayley, David H., and Egon Bittner. 1984. "Learning the Skills of Policing." *Law and Contemporary Problems* 47 (4): 36–59.

Bayley, David H., and James Garofalo. 1989. "The Management of Violence by Police Patrol Officers." *Criminology* 27 (1): 1–26.

Bittner, Egon. 1967. "The Police on Skid-Row: A Study of Peace-Keeping." *American Sociological Review* 32 (5): 699–715.

Bittner, Egon. 1974. "Florence Nightingale in Pursuit of Willie Sutton: A Theory of Police." In *The Potential Reform of Criminal Justice*, edited by H. Jacob, 17–34. Beverly Hills, CA: Sage.

Bittner, Egon. 1983. "Legality and Workmanship." In *Introduction in Control in the Police Organization*, edited by Maurice Punch, 1–11. Cambridge, MA: MIT Press.

Brown, Michael K. 1981. *Police Discretion and the Dilemmas of Reform*. New York: Russell Sage.

Campeau, Holly. 2015. "'Police Culture' at Work: Making Sense of Police Oversight." *British Journal of Criminology* 55: 669–687. doi:http://dx.doi.org/10.1093/bjc/azu093.

Chan, Janet. 1996. "Changing Police Culture." *British Journal of Criminology* 36 (1): 109–134.

Chan, Janet. 2007. "Making Sense of Police Reforms." *Theoretical Criminology* 11 (3): 323–345.

Civil Rights Division, U.S. Department of Justice. 2015. *Investigation of the Ferguson Police Department*. Washington, DC: U.S. Department of Justice.

Cockcroft, Tom. 2013. *Police Culture: Themes and Concepts*. London: Routledge.

Edwards, M. T., and E. M. Benjamin. 2009. "The Process of Peer Review in U.S. Hospitals." *Journal of Clinical Outcomes Management* 16 (10): 461–467.

Fielding, Nigel. 1984. "Police Socialization and Police Competence." *British Journal of Sociology* 35 (4): 568–590.

Goldstein, Herman. 1990. *Problem-Oriented Policing*. New York: McGraw-Hill.

Herbert, Steve. 1998. "Police Subculture Reconsidered." *Criminology* 36 (2): 343–370.

Jonathan-Zamir, Tal, Stephen D. Mastrofski, and Shomron Moyal. 2015. "Measuring Procedural Justice in Police-Citizen Encounters." *Justice Quarterly* 32 (5): 845–871.

Kahneman, Daniel. 2011. *Thinking Fast and Thinking Slow*. New York: Farrar, Strauss and Giroux.

Kelling, George L. 1999. *"Broken Windows" and Police Discretion*. Washington, DC: National Institute of Justice.

Law Enforcement Management and Administrative Statistics. 2013. Washington, DC: U.S. Department of Justice. Office of Justice Programs, Bureau of Justice Statistics.

Loftus, Bethan. 2009. *Police Culture in a Changing World*. Oxford: Oxford University Press.

Loftus, Bethan. 2010. "Police Occupational Culture: Classic Themes, Altered times." *Policing and Society* 20 (1): 1–20.

Lum, Cynthia. 2009. "Translating Police Research into Practice." In *Ideas in American Policing*, No. 11. Washington, DC: Police Foundation.

Manning, Peter K. 1977. *The Social Organization of Policing*. Cambridge, MA: MIT Press.

Mastrofski, Stephen D. 1996. "Measuring Police Performance in Public Encounters." In *Quantifying Quality in Policing*, edited by Larry T. Hoover, 207–241. Washington, DC: Police Executive Research Forum.

Mastrofski, Stephen D., James J. Willis, and Jeffrey B. Snipes. 2002. "Styles of Policing in a Community Policing Context." In *The Move to Community Policing: Making Change Happen*, edited by Merry Morash and J. Kevin Ford, 81–111. Thousand Oaks, CA: Sage.

Mastrofski, Stephen, and James J. Willis. 2010. "Police Organization Continuity and Change: Into the Twenty-First Century." In *Crime and Justice: A Review of Research*, edited by Michael Tonry, 55–144. Chicago, IL: University of Chicago Press.

Mastrofski, Stephen D. 2015. "Ideas and Insights: Police CEOs: Agents of Change?" *The Police Chief* 82 (November): 53–54.

Miller, Susan L. 1999. *Gender and Community Policing: Walking the Talk*. Boston, MA: Northeastern University Press.

Muir Jr, William K. 1977. *Police: Streetcorner Politicians*. Chicago, IL: University of Chicago Press.

National Research Council. 2004. *Fairness and Effectiveness in Policing: The Evidence*. Washington, DC: The National Academies Press.

Niederhoffer, Arthur. 1967. *Behind the Shield: Police in Urban Society*. New York: Doubleday and Company.

O'Neill, Megan, Monique Marks, and Anne-Marie Singh. 2007. *Police Occupational Culture: New Debates and Directions*. San Diego, CA: Elsevier, JAI.

Paoline, Eugene A., III. 2001. *Rethinking Police Culture: Officers' Occupational Attitudes*. New York: LFB Scholarly Publishing.

Paoline, Eugene A., III. 2003. "Taking Stock: Toward a Richer Understanding of Police Culture." *Journal of Crime and Justice* 31: 199–214.

Paoline, Eugene A., III. 2004. "Shedding Light on Police Culture: An Examination of Officers' Occupational Attitudes." *Police Quarterly* 7 (2): 205–236.

Paoline, Eugene A., III, Stephanie M. Myers, and Robert E. Worden. 2000. "Police Culture, Individualism, and Community Policing: Evidence from Two Police Departments." *Justice Quarterly* 17 (3): 575–605.

Paoline, Eugene A., III, Stephanie M. Myers, and Robert E. Worden. 2006. "Police Culture, Individualism, and Community Policing: Evidence from Two Departments." *Justice Quarterly* 17 (3): 575–605.

Paoline Eugene A., III, and William Terrill. 2014. *Police Culture: Adapting to the Strains of the Job*. Durham, NC: Carolina Academic Press.

President's Task Force on 21st Century Policing. 2015. *Final Report of the President's Task Force on 21st Century Policing*. Washington, DC: Office of Community Oriented Policing Services.

Rahr, Sue and Stephen K. Rice. 2015. *"From Warriors to Guardians: Recommitting American Police Culture to Democratic Ideals."* New Perspectives in Policing Bulletin. Washington, DC: U.S. Department of Justice, National Institute of Justice.

Reaves, Brian A. 2015. *Local Police Departments, 2013: Personnel, Policies and Practices*. Washington, DC: Bureau of Justice Statistics.

Reiner, Robert. 1978. *The Blue-Coated Work*. Cambridge: Cambridge University Press.

Reiner, Robert. 1985. *The Politics of the Police*. Brighton: Wheatsheaf Books.

Reiss Jr, Albert J. 1992. "Police Organization in the Twentieth Century." In *Modern Policing*, edited by Michael Tonry and Norval Morris, 51–97. Chicago, IL: University of Chicago Press.

Reuss-Ianni, Elizabeth. 1983. *Two Cultures of Policing: Street Cops and Management Cops*. New Brunswick, NJ: Transaction Publishers.

Rubinstein, Jonathan. 1973. *City Police*. New York: Farrar, Straus and Giroux.

Schon, D. A. 1983. *The Reflective Practitioner: How Professionals Think in Action*. New York: Basic Books.

Sherman, Lawrence W. 2013. "The Rise of Evidence-Based Policing: Targeting, Testing, and Tracking." *Crime and Justice* 42 (1): 377–451.

Sherman, Lawrence W. 2015. "A Tipping Point for 'Totally Evidenced Policing:' Ten Ideas for Building an Evidence-Based Police Agency." *International Criminal Justice Review* 25 (1): 11–29.

Sklansky, David. 2006. "Not Your Father's Police Department: Making Sense of the New Demographics of Law Enforcement." *Journal of Criminal Law and Criminology* 96 (3): 1209–1243.

Skolnick, Jerome H. 1966. *Justice without Trial: Law Enforcement in Democratic Society*. New York: Wiley.

Skolnick, Jerome H., and James. J. Fyfe. 1994. *Above the Law: Police and the Excessive Use of Force*. New York: The Free Press.

Telep, Cody. 2016. "Expanding the Scope of Evidence-Based Policing." *Criminology and Public Policy* 15 (1): 243–252.

Thacher, David. 2001. "Policing is Not a Treatment: Alternatives to the Medical Model of Police Research." *Journal of Research in Crime and Delinquency* 38 (4): 387–415.

Thacher, David. 2008. "Research for the Front Lines." *Policing and Society* 18 (1): 46–59.

Tyler, Tom R. 2004. "Enhancing Police Legitimacy." *The Annals of the American Academy of Political and Social Science* 593 (1): 84–99.

Van Maanen, John. 1974. "Working the Street: A Developmental View of Police Behavior." In *The Potential for Reform of Criminal Justice*, edited by Herbert Jacob, 83–130. Thousand Oaks, CA: Sage.

Westley, Westley A. 1953. "Violence and the Police." *American Journal of Sociology* 59 (1): 34–41.

Westley, Westley A. 1956. "Secrecy and the Police." *Journal of Social Forces* 34: 254–257.

Westley, W. A. 1970. *Violence and the Police: A Sociological Study of Law, Custom, and Morality*. Boston, MA: MIT Press.

Weisburd, David, and Anthony A. Braga, eds. 2006. *Police Innovation: Contrasting Perspectives*. New York: Cambridge University Press.

Weisburd, David, and Peter Neyroud. 2011. *Policing Science: Toward a New Paradigm*. Harvard Executive Session. Cambridge, MA: Harvard.

Willis, James J., Stephen D. Mastrofski, and David Weisburd. 2007. "Making Sense of Compstat: A Theory-Based Analysis of Organizational Change in Three Police Departments." *Law and Society Review* 41 (1): 147–188.

Willis, James J., and Stephen D. Mastrofski. 2016. "Improving Policing by Integrating Craft and Science: What Can Patrol Officers Teach Us about Good Police Work?" *Policing and Society*: 1–18. doi:http://dx.doi.org/10.1080/10439463.2015.1135921.

Wilson, James Q. 1968. *Varieties of Police Behavior*. Cambridge, MA: Harvard University Press.

Worden, Robert E. 1995. "Police Officers' Belief Systems: A Framework for Analysis." *American Journal of Police* 14 (1): 49–81.

Index

For Product Safety Concerns and Information please contact our EU
representative GPSR@taylorandfrancis.com
Taylor & Francis Verlag GmbH, Kaufingerstraße 24, 80331 München, Germany